KENT MU...

Other titles in this series include:

SURREY MURDERS
John Janaway
NORTHAMPTONSHIRE MURDERS
Paul Harrison
WARWICKSHIRE MURDERS
Betty Smith
MURDERS OF OLD SUSSEX
Rupert Taylor
YORKSHIRE MURDERS
Paul Harrison

KENT MURDERS

Alan Bignell

COUNTRYSIDE BOOKS
NEWBURY, BERKSHIRE

Produced through MRM Associates Ltd., Reading
Typeset by Acorn Bookwork, Salisbury
Printed in England by J.W. Arrowsmith Ltd, Bristol

Contents

Introduction   6

 1. The Bossenden Wood Murder   14

 2. The Rat-catcher's Wife   23

 3. The Cobham Woods Murder   30

 4. The Soldier's Farewell   38

 5. Poor Fanny Wallace   47

 6. The Jilted Suitor   53

 7. The Cain and Abel Killer   59

 8. Murder on The Lines   67

 9. A Born Loser   76

10. A Woman Scorned   90

11. Jailhouse Murder   99

12. The Dover Priory Murder   102

13. The Body in the Barn   109

14. The Bride in the Bath   116

Index   124

WITH MALICE
AFORETHOUGHT

K ENT has had its share of murders over the years. The crime
is one that has always excited special public interest and,
indeed, until about 150 years ago, public executions of
murderers drew crowds of several thousands, many of them
women and children, who brought to the scene much of the
atmosphere of a fairground.

Hardened execution-goers would speculate about how this
hanging would compare with others they had seen and some of
the sensation-seekers travelled (and that usually meant they
walked) many miles to witness the last moments of mortality of a
convicted murderer.

There was often a holiday spirit about the whole event, with
vendors offering their wares for sale among the crowd and pick-
pockets and thieves of all kinds regarded a well-attended execution as a welcome bonus to their annual income.

Because it was in Kent that the first Anglo-Saxon kingdom was
established, the county claims to be the birthplace of the English
nation and it could be said that that birth was conceived in
murder.

The Jutes who came from northern Germany and settled in the
Isle of Thanet under their leaders Hengist and Horsa in AD 449
soon tired of being hired mercenaries serving the British King
Vortigern. They determined that if they were going to fight for
anyone it might as well be for themselves and they treacherously
murdered many of the king's henchmen and put the rest to flight
in order to take over the kingdom for themselves.

One of the heirs to that kingdom was a king called Egbert, who might have merged fairly unobtrusively into the background of English history, as many of the other Saxon kings did, if he had not been persuaded that two of his young cousins were plotting to overthrow him and usurp his throne.

According to legend rather than recorded history, Egbert thwarted any possibility of that by having the two young princes murdered and buried in his royal palace at Eastry, near Sandwich in east Kent. The legend claims that the crime was brought to light in an unusually literal manner when a miraculous beam of light illuminated their grave and led to the discovery of their bodies.

The one murder in Kent that achieved national and even international renown was that which rocked Christendom in December 1170, when Archbishop Thomas Becket was murdered in his own cathedral at Canterbury by four knights who thought they were carrying out the wishes of Henry II, who was in France at the time.

No other murder in the whole of English history, perhaps, had quite such a profound effect as that one did. It not only reverberated through future church-state relations in England but it also founded a 400 year period of great prosperity for Canterbury, city as well as Cathedral. It was indirectly responsible for endowing English literature with one of its most enduring gems, Chaucer's Canterbury Tales, as well as a more recent classic, T.S. Eliot's Murder in the Cathedral.

Not too many murder victims can claim such distinction. Few, indeed, are even remembered for as long as their killers are. The murderers of Becket were never brought to human justice though they may well have gone to their graves convinced that their punishment would be of longer duration than that endured by most murderers. Because their crime was committed in church, they were subject only to church law and although they fled the kingdom their punishment was excommunication with its implied perpetual damnation.

Another historic murder was committed in the north Kent port of Faversham on the day after St Valentine's Day in 1551. Then, a former mayor of Faversham, Thomas Arden, was killed by his wife, her lover and their accomplices and the crime created enough of a stir in the county and beyond to become the inspiration for

The murder of Thomas Arden of Faversham by his wife and hired assassins, February, 1551.

the first domestic tragedy in English drama, possibly penned by William Shakespeare or Christopher Marlowe, although no-one knows for sure who wrote it.

The play is still performed occasionally. Simply called Arden (or Ardern) of Faversham, the plot, which closely followed historical fact, told how Alice Arden fell in love with a tailor called Thomas Mosby and plotted with him to murder her husband.

In the play, there follows a succession of sometimes near-farcical and always unsuccessful attempts upon Arden's life by three hired assassins called Black Will, Shakebag and John Green, with the help of a servant called Michael Sanderson who is enticed into the plot by the promise of marriage to Mosby's sister, Susan. Others were also involved.

At last, the bunglers succeed and while their victim plays a board game in his own parlour with Mosby, the rest of the murderous crew leap from hiding and poor Arden is hit with a tailor's pressing iron, strangled and stabbed, his wife delivering the final, fatal blow.

The disposal of the body was achieved with as little finesse as the murder. It was carried from the house, footprints were left in freshly fallen snow that led to a field behind the house and blood was left spattered on the floor inside the house. Questions were asked almost immediately by visitors who arrived, by Arden's invitation, only minutes after the deed was done and soon the plotters were all informing on each other so that in very little time most of those involved were in custody.

Trial, condemnation and execution followed with similar despatch. Alice Arden was burned to death at Canterbury, and Thomas Mosby and his sister were hanged at Smithfield in London. Elizabeth Stafford, one of the servants in the Arden household, was accused of being an 'abetter and counsellor to the murder' and was burned at Faversham, where Michael Sanderson and John Green were hanged. George Bradshaw, the Faversham goldsmith who introduced the hired assassin Black Will to Alice Arden, was hanged at Canterbury.

Black Will was eventually brought to justice in Flushing, in the Low Countries, where he, too, was burned to death.

Arden's House, now substantially altered inside, is still to be seen in Faversham's picturesque Abbey Street.

If Thomas Arden had been a less prominent member of his local community, his murder would, no doubt, have been forgotten as quickly as most domestic homicides are. Murder, after all, is more commonly committed within the family than outside it.

Until the middle of the 18th century, assizes, at which most murder trails were heard, were held in various towns in Kent, including Canterbury, Dartford, Gravesend, Sevenoaks and Greenwich. The last Kent Assize to be held at Canterbury was in 1741 and by 1758 all assizes were being held in the county town of Maidstone.

The town had its own gaol at the top of the High Street until the new county gaol was opened in what is now King Street, in 1746. It was too small from the start and conditions were appalling, especially during assizes when the occupancy could double and prisoners had to be held in churches and chapels and other public buildings while they waited for sentencing.

At last, in 1810, a 15 acre site was bought for another new prison, this time at the top end of Week Street. It was completed in 1819 and 141 prisoners were transferred there in March that year.

The new Sessions House was added, adjoining the prison, in 1826 and after 1827 all Kent assizes were held there. The Sessions House is now incorporated into the 20th century County Hall block. Assizes ended in 1971 and the old Sessions House courts were vacated in favour of a new crown court, served by high court and circuit judges, on a prominent site beside the river in the centre of the town. Kent County Council then took over the courts' former premises and converted them for its own purposes.

Until 1831, executions were carried out in public on Penenden Heath, an area of heathland just outside Maidstone, and condemned prisoners were taken by horsedrawn cart through the town to the gallows there, usually accompanied by a large, noisy procession of ghoulish spectators.

The gallows had already been moved in 1813 to a less prominent site on Penenden Heath where the melancholy spectacle would be less visible in the landscape and would not be seen at all from houses in nearby Boxley village.

But in 1819 eleven Penenden Heath landowners and residents

The new Sessions House built adjoining the prison at Maidstone in 1826. Kent assizes were held there from 1827.

petitioned Kent magistrates to remove the place of execution to the front of the new gaol, a site more in keeping with practices in most English towns by this time. The petitioners were less concerned with the ghoulishness of the spectacle than with their property, which they complained was being damaged by the mobs that attended the executions, trampling down their hedges and crops.

Nothing was done, however, until 1831 when the High Sheriff of Kent, responding to an appeal by Lord Baden Powell, told the county justices at their meeting in June: '. . . there are great objections to the sentence of death being carried into effect at Penenden Heath, not only as it affects the morals of the persons who are drawn to witness the execution, by many of whom it seems rather to be considered as affording an opportunity for dissipation and vice than as presenting an awful and salutary warning, but especially as it affects the unhappy criminal whose mind is too frequently distracted during the procession of not less than a mile from that attention to his spiritual adviser to which the last hours of his life ought to be continually devoted . . .'

As a result, orders were given for future executions to take place on the roof of the gaol entrance lodge. It meant an end to the unruly processions through the town and it also meant the crowds, sometimes several thousand strong, who still gathered in the open area between the prison and the town, could be more easily controlled.

Later, the scaffold was re-sited beside the porter's lodge, close to the present public entrance to County Hall, at street level and after 1865 it was hung round with black crepe so that when the condemned criminal fell to his death, only the top of his head remained visible to the spectators.

The first of the prison hangings was in August 1831, when John Any Bird Bell died for the murder of another boy at Chatham. Altogether, 26 men and two women died in public hangings at Maidstone prison before the Capital Punishment Act of 1868 ended the practice. After that, murderers were executed inside the gaol walls until Britain abolished capital punishment (except for treason) in 1965.

Many of the murderers who were brought to trial during the

Early members of Kent County Constabulary, which was formed in 1857 (Picture: Kent Police Museum).

19th century had given themselves up or made very little effort to disguise their crime. It is beyond doubt that more sophisticated murders were committed and never brought to light because police methods were still very crude and it did not demand very great ingenuity to make them ineffective.

Early police forces recruited their officers 'by the pound' rather than for any scholarly or other achievements. If they were big enough to look after themselves in a fracas and strong enough to deal with any ruffian who tried to resist arrest, they were in. They were not obliged to be literate and they had no formal training of any kind, learning the job by going out as probationers for a period with more experienced officers.

They had no transport, other than their own two feet, and no means of communicating with distant colleagues other than their whistles, with the possibility of recourse to the public telegraph for very special emergencies.

It was not until 1857 that Kent County Constabulary was

formed under the command of Captain John Hay Ruxton, who was selected for the job of first Chief Constable of Kent by the county justices at General Sessions.

At that time there were already a number of city and borough police forces, usually very small, and it was only the areas not covered by these local forces that became the responsibility of the 220 officers of the new county force.

In his first General Order to the new force, Capt Ruxton asked all his officers to work for the 'grand aim and object of the County Constabulary ... the prevention of crime and the maintenance of good order.'

The county force had its headquarters at Wren's Cross in Upper Stone Street, Maidstone, but by the 1930s it had outgrown those premises and a new site in Sutton Road was bought. The main building of the new headquarters was brought into use in 1940.

Although the first detective branch was formed in 1896, it had only one detective sergeant and three detective constables to cover the whole county.

Today, the Kent police force is one of the largest and best-equipped in the country and it is still carrying out the spirit of that first General Order of its first Chief Constable and aiming to prevent crime and maintain good order.

Although the law no longer demands the death penalty for murder, the crime retains its fascination, in fact as well as in fiction. It is still the ultimate crime, to which men and women may be driven by any one or a combination of emotions: love or hate, anger or sorrow, fear, despair, even compassion and, most tragically of all perhaps, sometimes no rational reason whatever.

All but one of the murders featured in this book were committed, in Kent, during the 19th century. They span the period during which executions were first fully public, then partly veiled from the spectators and finally confined to within the prison walls.

Some of them are quite celebrated cases, for one reason or another. Some are surrounded with drama and incident that affected whole communities; others, sad little tragedies of personal relationships that touched few beyond the immediate protagonists – in fact, a typical selection of murders committed anywhere at any time.

THE BOSSENDEN WOOD MURDER

O NE of the strangest – certainly one of the most colourful – of Kentish murderers was a man who called himself Sir William Courtenay but who is probably better known by the name his eccentricities earned him: Mad Thom.

He had other names, too. He was born John Nicholas Thom, son of a Cornish publican. When he first came to public notice in Kent it was as Count Rothschild, the name under which he stayed at a Canterbury inn in 1832.

But it was as Lord Viscount William Courtenay of Powderham that he stood for Parliament in Canterbury: a colourful figure who dressed in elaborate style and carried a sword with which he threatened anyone who heckled him when he addressed his electorate.

He supported the Reform Bill, won 374 votes and four years in Barming Asylum after he was accused of perjury. His father appealed against his continued incarceration at the end of that time and Queen Victoria was 'graciously pleased to extend her grace and mercy' to him. It was not, perhaps, the kindness it was meant to be.

Courtenay, as he was now known, returned to Canterbury imbued with a campaigning zeal to improve the conditions of the local agricultural labourers. If he could not do it in Parliament then, he determined, he would do it in the countryside, among the people he was resolved to help.

Soon he was going among them, declaring himself to be Christ reincarnated, saviour of the common man. He even exhibited the

Sir William Courtenay, alias John Thom, on his favourite charger (from *The Penny Satirist*, 1838).

marks of the Crucifixion nails on his hands and such was his magnetic personality and the power of his oratory that he quickly gathered a small band of convinced 'disciples' who he 'baptised' at Waterham Well near Canterbury to make them, he promised, invulnerable.

Then, mounted on a white horse and armed with pistols and a great cavalry sword, and with a blue and white standard on which some of his women followers had painted a rampant lion, he headed a growing procession that wandered fairly aimlessly about the neighbourhood for several days, recruiting more followers from among the field workers they passed.

His recruiting methods included giving away bread and sometimes cheese and promising to every man who joined him a share in the land ownership redistribution that was to follow his dismantlement of the great estates.

The desertion of the workers to follow him caused problems for their employers of course, and in the end one Hernhill farmer (a Mr Curling) decided enough was enough. He asked the authorities in Canterbury to arrest the deserters and restrain Courtenay from further abductions.

At about 9am on Tuesday, May 29, 1838 the ragged company following Courtenay – about 45 men and women – was at Boughton under Blean, between Canterbury and Faversham. There, Courtenay bought some bread and they all went into the house of a local man called William Wills, where he told them: 'This is the 29th May and a glorious 29th May it shall be for the poor who stick by me. They have been long enough imposed upon and I will lead them through it.'

The company shared a bread and cheese meal together and then Courtenay sent out for some tobacco which he also shared among them, while some of the women sang to them.

Courtenay sent the men out to get some good big boughs which they could use as clubs and at 11am they all left the house, Wills carrying the banner and Courtenay himself with a symbolic loaf of bread carried aloft on the end of a stick.

Sir William had discarded his finery for a brown Holland frock and overalls, belted with a leather belt into which were stuck a brace of pistols and from which hung his cavalry sword in its steel scabbard. Round his neck was hung a trumpet.

He fell in the men, military style, in threes and then sounding the trumpet he marched them off.

Whether or not he had any clearer idea of the destination of this day's march than he had before is not known, but after some time they found themselves at a farmhouse where there was a pond with a hop garden nearby.

One man was detailed to take Sir William's white horse and go to Graveney church, on the marshes between Whitstable and Faversham, where he was to gather as many men as he could. The rest of the little 'army' went on into a nearby cornfield where Courtenay left them while he went to a beanstack on the edge of the hop garden. They thought he was going to set fire to it, and perhaps that was his intention, but after a while he returned to tell them: 'I am now going to strike the bloody blow; the streets that have heretofore flowed with water shall flow with blood for the rise of the poor.'

The bemused band spent the rest of that day marching through the parishes and villages of Eastling, Throwley, Sheldwich Lees and Selling and eventually, on Wednesday evening, they arrived at Mr Culver's Bossenden Farm at Dunkirk, roughly midway between Faversham and Canterbury.

The Canterbury magistrates had, by this time, received the plea from Farmer Curling and issued warrants for Courtenay's arrest. On Thursday morning, May 31, Constable John Mears was sent to make the arrest and he took with him his brother, Nicholas, a Boughton plumber. Both knew that they could not expect their job to be done without some danger to themselves so Nicholas insisted that he would be the one to approach Courtenay since if the worst happened, he at least would not leave any children.

Meanwhile, Courtenay addressed his followers.

'This is the Day of Judgment,' he told them. 'This the first day of the millennium and this day I will put the crown on my head. Behold, a greater than Sampson is with you. If any of you wish to go home, you may have my permission to go, but if you desert me, I will follow you to the furthermost parts of hell and invoke fire and brimstone from heaven upon you!'

When the two brothers reached Bossenden at between 7am and

8am, Nicholas Mears went forward to serve the warrant. Courtenay came to meet him.

'Are you the constable?' he asked. Mears said he was, whereupon Courtenay shot him. Then, drawing his sword, he slashed at him and as Mears lay on the ground, dead or dying, Courtenay kicked him. Then he turned away contemptuously and ordered his men to throw the body into a nearby ditch.

After the murder of Nicholas Mears, the little band followed Thom into the house of one of his 'disciples', a man called Hadlow, where Thom paid for bread and cheese for all and administered a sacrament which, he promised, would make them invincible in the coming confrontation.

He preached a sermon to them in which he renewed his promise of 30 or 40 acres for each man and told them he had come among them on a cloud and on a cloud he would be taken away again and no bullet or other weapon could harm him.

He told them: 'If 10,000 soldiers came against me, they would turn aside or fall dead at my command.'

News of the murder of Mears reached Canterbury before 11.30am and 100 men of the 45th Foot Regiment stationed there were hurriedly dispatched to Dunkirk to deal with Thom and his men. When Thom heard of their coming, he led his men out into an open field which he decided should be the battlefield.

The soldiers were accompanied by several of the county magistrates and the detail split into two groups to come upon the rioters from two sides. Some of Thom's men, seeing the soldiers, decided that discretion was much the better part of valour and melted back into anonymity in the countryside, but most stayed.

Thom, seeing the strength of the force sent against him, chose to withdraw his own slightly smaller force into nearby Bossenden Wood and it was there he took his final stand.

The first casualty of the battle that followed was Lt Bennett, who approached Thom and called upon him to surrender. Thom responded by shooting him dead. One of the lieutenant's men, who had his gun aimed at Thom, killed him instantly.

Desperately, the mob charged the soldiers. Eight of them were killed, another seven or eight severely wounded and a dozen or so were taken prisoner. The rest fled. As well as the lieutenant, one other officer was severely wounded and four or five privates were seriously injured. One later died.

By 7pm, the soldiers were back in Canterbury with their prisoners. The Battle of Bossenden Wood was over.

The repercussions, however, were not. The dead were taken to the Red Lion inn in Boughton Street where they were laid out for formal identification. Within minutes, pieces were being torn from Thom's clothing as relics by still-faithful devotees and as souvenirs by others.

An inquest was held at the inn. Even as it was going on, three more of the severely wounded rioters died.

The coroner's jury returned a verdict of wilful murder of Nicholas Mears against William Courtenay, alias John Thom, and also against William Burford, William Price, Thomas Mears (cousin of the murdered Mears), Alexander Foad, and William Nutting.

Courtenay and Burford were both dead but the other four were all committed on the coroner's warrant to Maidstone gaol to await trial.

There was a separate inquest on Lt Bennett, at which the jury unanimously returned a verdict of wilful murder against Courtenay and also Edward Wraight (snr), Edward Wraight (jnr), Thomas Mears, James Goodwin, William Wills, William Foster, Henry Hadlow, Alexander Foad, Phineas Harvey, John Spratt, Stephen Baker, William Burford, Thomas Griggs, John Silk, George Blanchard, Edward Curling, George Griggs, William Rye and Richard Foreman. All of them who could be were removed to Maidstone gaol.

The assizes opened on Tuesday, August 7, 1838 and the men were tried by none less than the Lord Chief Justice of England himself, Lord Denman, who had a reputation for being a very fair judge.

The grand jury decided that only Price and Mears should stand trial for the murder of Nicholas Mears and Wills, Wraights Snr and Jnr, Foad, Curling, Griggs, Charles Hills, Foreman and Mears for the murder of Lt Bennett. The rest were discharged.

Price and Mears were tried first on Thursday, August 9. Mears was 29 and he appeared in court wearing a sailor's jacket, a blue waistcoat and dark trousers. He was described as a man with a fair complexion, auburn hair and whiskers and lively blue eyes. He was regarded as something of a religious fanatic. Price was 30, although he looked older. He was a much more hard-faced man, but neither of them looked as though they were particularly violent types.

The case was heard throughout the day. The courtroom was crowded and the public – many of whom were relatives of the accused men – listened attentively and apprehensively as Lord Denman embarked upon his summing up, which ended at 5pm. When the jury retired, a doctor was called to attend to Price, who was looking decidedly ill. He was soon restored however and returned to the dock before the jury returned at 5.30 with verdicts of guilty against both men, with a strong recommendation of mercy for both of them 'in consequence of the infatuated manner in which they were led astray by the unfortunate maniac Courtenay.'

Lord Denham passed the statutory death sentence but added 'I pass this sentence immediately that I may have the opportunity of adding that it will not be carried into effect and of assuring you that your lives will be spared in consequence of the merciful recommendation of the jury.'

The prisoners were led away, still not knowing what their punishment was to be.

On Friday, August 10, the other eight prisoners were tried. Foad appeared in the dock with a disfiguring face wound. All eight pleaded guilty and all were, in fact, found guilty but again Lord Denman pronounced the death sentence and added: 'Having performed the duty which the law imposes upon me with regard to pronouncing the sentence, I do not think it right to keep you a moment in doubt as to its being carried into execution for having made up my mind on the question I think it right to state to you that your lives will be spared.

'Your offence is of an enormous nature and I think that along with the fanaticism and folly which have marked your acts, there has been so much bad feeling, there has been so much disregard to the happiness and safety of your fellow men, there has been so much recklessness, mischief and such a determined resolution not to interfere to prevent it when you all saw how imminent and frightful it was, that I have really felt it to be a very strong act on

Thomas Mears and William Price, two of the three who were transported for their part in the insurgency.

my part to come to the resolution that your lives should not be forfeited to the law.'

He went on to say that friends and relations of Lt Bennett had told him it would be the greatest aggravation of their sufferings for the loss of their son if any more blood was to be spilled in consequence of this unhappy affair.

The judge then told the prisoners what their fates would be.

Thomas Mears and William Wills were to be transported for life. William Price would be transported for ten years. Wraight, Foad, Curling, Griggs, Foreman and Hills would each serve one year's hard labour, with one month's solitary confinement.

Lord Denham then ordered Mrs Hadlow, mother of Henry Hadlow, to be brought to the bar, where he told her that her son had been committed on a charge of murder and, if tried, he would have been found guilty. However, the prosecution had dropped the charge against him because of his youth and the severe injuries he had sustained. But, he said, she had encouraged Courtenay and it was her fault that Henry was led into 'this horrible and dangerous transaction'.

The judge told her: 'You ought to thank God he has escaped from its penalty and take care you do not of your example lead others into like activation.'

Mrs Hadlow then left the court, apparently still fanatically convinced of the inherent righteousness of Sir William Courtenay's cause.

After the assizes were over, the Mayor of Faversham, Edward Crowe, sponsored a petition asking for a review of the sentences of Mears, Price and Wills, which he and his supporters regarded as unnecessarily severe in the circumstances. But Home Secretary Lord John Russell refused to interfere and the three men were transported to Australia. None ever returned to England.

Mears and Wills earned remission for good behaviour and Mears became a gold miner and apparently prospered. Only Wills tried to return to England. He wrote to the vicar of Hernhill, the Rev C.R. Handley, in 1852 asking his advice about whether he should return or not. The vicar advised him that it would probably be best all round if he did not return without an absolute pardon and Wills took the advice.

The cause of it all, Mad Thom himself, was buried with very little ceremony in the churchyard at Hernhill, in an unmarked grave with no mound so that the body and the site should be safe from the many people who still believed he was the embodiment of the Second Coming.

The whole dramatic episode was a consequence of the harshness of life for the rural dwellers who were beginning to agitate for improvements in their working conditions and their standard of living, both of which Thom promised them.

The countryside around the hamlet of Dunkirk, high on the downs between Canterbury and Boughton, was still very sparsely populated and relatively lawless. An inquiry into the causes of the Courtenay riots found that there was no church to provide any kind of moral leadership for the malcontents, many of whom were involved in smuggling to boost their meagre incomes, and virtually no exercise of any law at all.

In fact, it was as a direct result of the William Courtenay affair that Dunkirk church was built and it stands today as the only monument, albeit an unintentional one, to Mad Thom; a man whose eccentricity (if not, in fact, his actual madness) led the followers who accepted him as their saviour or even, some of them, as The Saviour, to murder rather than the glorious millennium he promised them.

THE RAT-CATCHER'S WIFE

A STRANGER to Kent would have difficulty in locating Otterden today. It isn't marked on most maps and even if you did find it, up there on the North Downs west of Charing Hill, the chances are you would go through it without even noticing it.

It was a no more significant place in 1839, when farmer Henry Jenkins left his house there one Saturday mid-day to go to a wedding. He left his children at home on their own, but he arranged for a neighbour, Hannah Giles, wife of the local rat-catcher, to come in at about 7pm and to stay until he returned.

Mrs Giles, a woman of about 42, had often come to look after the house for Mr Jenkins whenever he was away from home and he had no qualms about her reliability.

It had been snowing when he left home; not specially hard, but enough to leave tracks as he walked along the road towards his father's house. His way took him past the Giles' home and as he passed he saw coming out of the garden gate a man he knew to be Samuel Seager.

The two men exchanged a few words. Jenkins was not surprised to see Seager leaving the Giles' house. He had often seen him there before and it was common knowledge anyway that Seager quite often paid a visit to Hannah Giles, usually when her husband was out.

Seager was a widower; the youngest of nine sons of a small farmer. Although he lived at Stalisfield, a few miles from Otterden, he carried on the business of shoemaker at his mother's house in

Otterden and for about a year Hannah had worked with him, helping him with his shoemaking. The two had been – well, good friends, at least since the summer of 1837. Their friendship caused a lot of gossip in the parish and Hannah's husband had, in fact, banned Seager from visiting her at home in an effort to still the nagging tongues.

Farmer Jenkins had a brother who lived next door to the Gileses and he knew as well as anyone that Seager was, nevertheless, in the habit of visiting Hannah in her home, banned or not.

That Saturday, Seager went to one of the other neighbours, Elizabeth Roberts, some time between 9 and 10am, to ask her if the Gileses were at home. Mrs Roberts told him she had heard her neighbours indoors and Seager stood near the cottage window where he could watch the Giles' cottage.

Eventually, he left and when Mrs Roberts went to call on Mrs Giles about an hour later, there, sure enough, was Seager. Two of the Giles children, eight year old Jane and eleven year old Stephen, were in the same room with them.

When Mrs Roberts arrived, Seager got up and left almost at once to go to his mother's house nearby, and it wasn't long after that that he was seen by another woman, Ann Harris, to be melting down some lead in an iron spoon and using a potato from which he had gouged some moulds to make bullets for a pistol he had.

Seager had, in fact, bought the pistol from a Stalisfield blacksmith some eight months before and had lent it to one of the local farm workers, a man called Henry Chapman, on January 30. More recently, he had sent his eldest son to get it back and now his two sons, aged five and seven, were watching him as he cast the lead into bullets for the gun.

Seager's mother wished he would give the pistol to her. Indeed, she begged him to do so, but he wouldn't, not even when Mrs Harris, during her visit, joined in. His mother actually went on her knees to him, begging him to hand over the weapon to her, but he still would not.

In the end, the bullets cast, Seager went out, taking the pistol and the bullets with him, leaving the two women standing at the cottage door and watching him walk off through the snow towards Charing.

Hannah, meanwhile, left her own cottage some time before 6pm while her own son, eight year old James, was at the shops. When he got back, his mother had left the house. He knew she was due to baby sit for Mr Jenkins and would sleep at the Jenkins house and he settled himself down for the night.

During the evening, he heard a pistol fired and he heard two screams, but he did not connect either with his mother and he went on getting some supper for himself and his older brother, Stephen, after which both boys went to bed.

Henry Jenkins, 13 year old son of farmer Jenkins, was at home with his brothers and sisters, waiting for Hannah Giles to arrive. He, too, heard the shot and he went outside and called their dog in, in case someone was shooting at it. As he opened the door to call the dog, he smelled burning, but it didn't seem to be near enough to cause alarm and he went back indoors.

The Jenkins children waited until nearly 8pm for Hannah to arrive and when she had not, Henry went out and walked a little way along the lane towards her cottage to see if she was coming.

About halfway to her house, he saw that something was smouldering at the roadside, near the hedge, about 20 yards from another house belonging to the Luckhurst family. Horrified, he thought he could make out the figure of a man with a fire burning on his chest. Too frightened to go any closer, young Henry turned and ran back home and locked the door.

His father did not return home until after 1am, but Henry was still waiting up for him with news of what he had seen.

Not sure whether to be angry with Hannah for failing to keep her promise to look after the house for him while he was away or concerned because, clearly, something was amiss, the farmer went with his eldest son back along the lane in the moonlight.

What they found was not the body of a man but of a woman – poor Hannah Giles. She had been shot four times, her throat had been cut and an attempt had been made to burn the body, which was lying some 100 yards from the Luckhurst house.

The farmer at once called out his brother, William, and

Hannah's husband, Stephen Giles, was called too. Together, they moved the body and they found, underneath it, a pistol.

Stephen Giles took possession of the weapon and also of a razor case which was found nearby. There were also a pair of scissors which he identified as belonging to his wife.

The men saw that, leading away from the body, a trail of footprints in the snow led to the house of Samuel Seager but of the shoemaker himself there was no trace.

Charles Wilks, a surgeon of Charing, was called to examine the body. He knew Hannah. He found a five inch throat wound that extended from front to spine and there were gunshot wounds on the thighs. A finger on each hand had been cut to the joints. Mr Wilks was in no doubt that death resulted from the throat wound which he decided must have been inflicted from behind.

The body was also badly burned on the thighs, abdomen, breast and arms in such a way as to indicate that the flames had burned from the lowest point to the uppermost.

Later that Sunday morning, Stephen Giles called for another neighbour, Henry Bushell, and together they went along the road until they found tracks showing that someone had crossed a field coming towards the Luckhurst house, apparently from the back part of the Giles' house.

Seager, meanwhile, had fled the county altogether and was living as a tramp. Rumour soon had an explanation for the events of that tragic Saturday night. It was said that Seager, not content with the friendship of Hannah Giles, had developed a passion for her which she rejected and he had killed her in a fit of jealous rage.

In fact, though, Seager was to tell a very different story.

Seager's description was circulated and on February 10, while he was looking for work on the railways at Coleshill near Birmingham, under the name of William Rogers, he was seen by local timber merchant and constable Charles Shuttleworth, who thought he recognised in Rogers the description of the man wanted for the Otterden murder in Kent.

Shuttleworth challenged Seager, who admitted his identity and then made a run for it. He did not get very far this time, though. He was again arrested by another Coleshill constable, Richard Peach, who took Seager into custody.

Even then, Seager almost cheated justice again, this time by attempting to strangle himself with his own bootlaces. He was unconscious when he was found, but he recovered and was duly returned to Kent where he was charged with the murder of Hannah Giles.

He admitted the crime. He claimed that what actually happened was that Hannah, trapped into an unhappy marriage with the rat-catcher, who was often away from home, had not rejected his advances and they became lovers. Then, when he formed a relationship with another woman, Hannah became jealous and made things difficult for him.

Seager was brought to trial at the Kent Lenten Assizes in March 1839. He appeared in the dock in the clothes he normally wore: a fustian shooting jacket with waistcoat and trousers of a similar material and with a pink and white check handkerchief round his neck. He was a fresh-faced man of about 30, with a mild expression, sandy hair and whiskers

In spite of having earlier admitted the crime, in court he pleaded not guilty to the charge of wilful murder of Hannah Giles.

Evidence was given at the trial by blacksmith Richard Benstead, who said he had put some steel 'specks' on a pair of shoes for Seager about three weeks before the murder. He recalled that the shoes were very distinctively crooked – in fact, he went so far as to say he didn't ever remember seeing another pair of shoes quite like them. After he heard about the murder he went to see the tracks made across the field and he had no doubt at all that those tracks were made by someone wearing those same crooked shoes of Seager's.

Those footprints all led away from the place where the body was found.

As well as the razor case found near the body, a razor was also found in a bit of woodland about 100 yards from the Luckhurst house. The razor was scrutinised by a Maidstone optician using a magnifying glass and was found to have marks upon it that could have been a mis-spelling of Seager's name, together with the word Otterden.

Another witness at the trial was Viscount Marsham, a magistrate, who visited Seager in gaol at the prisoner's request, and to whom Seager made a statement, which was written down for him, in which he said: 'I wish to say I did this crime. I did it and I wish it known. We had a few words and that was the reason of it.'

Seager's defence admitted he committed the crime but claimed it amounted to manslaughter, not murder. His lawyer dismissed the evidence of the crooked shoe-prints in the snow, saying there was no evidence they were made by Seager. The road was, after all, a public one and the tracks could have been made by anyone.

He suggested that the scissors found near the body could have indicated that Seager was provoked into attacking Hannah and he pointed out that no trace of blood was found on the razor, which might or might not have belonged to Seager anyway.

At the end of the hearing and the judge's summing up, the jury consulted together for about 15 minutes without leaving the courtroom, but were unable to agree a verdict and eventually retired to do so. They were out about half an hour and when they returned the foreman said they were reluctantly obliged to say the accused was guilty of murder.

The black cap was donned and the death sentence passed.

The trial had lasted from 9am until 7.15pm and Seager was said to have manifested the greatest composure throughout.

But the calmness was all outward show. In the last few days before his execution, Seager spent much of his time on his knees in his cell. Although he was not able to read well when he first went to prison, he improved a great deal as a result of the practice he had reading the Bible and other religious books.

At 11.45am on Thursday, March 28, 1839, Samuel Seager began his last walk from the condemned cell to the scaffold which had been built, as usual, over the entrance lodge to Maidstone prison. Precisely at noon he was led on to the platform, the noose was adjusted by the executioner, the bolt was drawn, and Samuel Seager paid the penalty for his crime.

The execution was witnessed by a crowd of several thousand people who had gathered outside the prison. Most of them were, as usual, women and children and while they waited for the condemned man to be brought to the platform there was a great deal of jostling and laughter and exchanges of recollections of the behaviour of other prisoners in the past and conjecture about how this one would conduct himself at the last.

One woman was overheard to complain, when the spectacle was over, that she had come eleven miles to see it and it was all over in two minutes.

Among the crowd on this occasion was the widowed husband of Hannah Giles, rat-catcher Stephen Giles. Some time before the prisoner was brought out, Giles was to be seen wearing a white smock with a black hat band and smoking his pipe, elbowing his way through the crowd to get as close to the gallows as he could.

When Seager was brought out, Giles made no secret of the fact that he couldn't wait to see him 'turned off', and when the lifeless body of his wife's murderer hung before him, Giles turned to another of the spectators standing beside him and remarked: '. . . him, he looks better now than ever I see him look in his life!'

THE COBHAM WOODS MURDER

THOUSANDS of people poured into the Medway Towns of Rochester and Chatham on Tuesday, August 29, 1843 in readiness for the big military display that was to be held on Chatham Lines that afternoon.

Among those who for business reasons were travelling in the opposite direction away from the Towns and cursing the crowds because of the traffic they brought and the delays they caused, were two Rochester butchers, Abraham Lester (or Lyster) and his nephew Charles Lester. They were going in their horse-drawn cart to Wrotham market, to buy livestock there.

Their way took them across the river Medway, through Strood and Cobham village – a route well-known to the writer Charles Dickens, incidentally, and to members of the Pickwick Club who were spectators at a very similar military spectacle during their excursion into Kent.

But before the two butchers reached the village, while they were still driving through Cobham Woods, part of the parkland surrounding the family home of the Earl of Darnley, Cobham Hall, they came across a man lying in a shallow hollow at the side of the road.

Charles nudged his uncle.

'He's had a drop too much, by the looks of him,' he guessed.

Abraham frowned.

'More than a drop, I'd say, to be lying like that, face down.'

Charles pulled the horse to a halt and climbed down.

'I'll just go over and see if he's all right,' he decided, and he went to where the man lay.

There was something about the man that did not seem quite right. He was of middle age, respectably dressed in a well-tailored dark suit and a green plaid waistcoat. Not the sort of person that would have been expected to have fallen on his face in a drunken stupor out here in the woods.

As Charles bent to turn the man over, he realised why he had thought this might not be just another drunk. This man was not dead drunk. He was just dead.

A shepherd, George Biggs, had been in the woods looking for some lost sheep and he came upon the little tableau just as Charles was about to turn the body over. He came closer.

'This man's dead,' Charles told him. 'See, his throat's been cut. There's blood everywhere. Give me a hand to turn him over, will you?'

Together, the two men turned the body on to its back and then they saw that, as well as having his throat cut, he had been stabbed several times. His clothes were torn and there was blood on his face and hands.

Charles went back to the cart and told his uncle what they had discovered.

'Best get on into Cobham, fast as we can, and fetch the constable,' Abraham decided and that, in fact, was just what they did.

The village constable was a man called William Dawes. He was a full-time tailor but when the Rochester butchers found him at his house and told him about the dead man in the woods, he assumed his part-time constabulary role and went directly to the scene of what was, obviously, a crime.

A search of the body and the surrounding area brought to light a large knife lying close to the body and a cut throat razor smeared with blood nearby. There were signs in the grass that a considerable struggle had taken place.

By now, news of the murder – for such it clearly was – had brought a small crowd of spectators to the scene and it was not long before any further clues there might have been were trampled out of sight. However, blood was found on a stile nearby and Dawes jumped to the conclusion that it must have been left there by Charles Lester as he left the body to hurry on to Cobham with news of his discovery.

The Ship inn at Cobham, where the body of Robert Dadd was brought and the inquest held.

It did not seem to occur to anyone at the time that it might also have been left there by the escaping killer.

One of the onlookers was John Adams, a waiter at The Ship inn at Cobham. He looked at the dead man and recognised him at once. He had known him as Robert Dadd before he retired as a Chatham chemist some time before. Dadd had then had a high street shop and had been a prominent townsman and political activist.

Adams told the constable: 'He came to The Ship last evening with his son, Richard, asking for a bed for the night. We didn't have a room with two beds but this man said the other was his son so it would be quite all right for them to sleep together.'

The constable ruled out robbery as a motive for the murder after he found three sovereigns and a gold watch among the victim's possessions. In the absence of the dead man's son, it did not tax even the very indifferent detective skills of the village constable to lead him to the conclusion that the man they needed to find was that very son, Richard Dadd.

Robert Dadd's body was carried back to Cobham and lodged in The Ship inn, where an inquest was held at which the waiter, John Adams said both men had gone for a walk together after their arrival at the inn the day before.

After they returned, the younger man went out again on his own and later still, at about 9pm, both men went out for another walk together. Adams waited up for their return until about 1am and then went to bed.

Having heard the evidence of the witnesses, the coroner told the jury that, from the circumstances of the case, they had not the slightest evidence to connect the son with the murder, although there might appear to be a great deal of suspicion. He considered the best and safest course for them to pursue would be to return a verdict of wilful murder against some person or persons unknown, which the jury duly did.

The inquest was attended by two of the deceased's sons and several other relatives and friends. Every room in the inn was filled with people, many of whom had known Robert Dadd when he had his chemist's shop. The spot where the body was found became an immediate tourist attraction and a great many people travelled from some distance away to see it.

As it happened, before Robert and his son left London, one of Richard's sisters wrote to her elder brother, who was visiting Strood, telling him of the proposed journey to Cobham, and expressing fears for their father's safety. That letter reached the brother only minutes before the news of the murder and he at once hurried to Cobham. He immediately decided Richard was the culprit and he arranged for a handbill to be printed, published and circulated, offering a £10 reward to any person finding or securing him.

Richard Dadd was not exactly an unknown. Born in 1817, son of his father's first marriage, he was educated in the Medway Towns where he distinguished himself as an unusually gifted artist. Indeed, it was his artistic talent that decided his father to leave Kent and move to London, so that Richard could study at the Royal Academy, where his ability won him some fame.

That fame, in turn, earned him an invitation to accompany Sir Thomas Phillips, a solicitor, on a grand tour of Europe and North

Africa, in order to draw some of the sights for his patron.

It was during the North African part of their journey together that Dadd first exhibited some distinctly odd behaviour. He claimed he had been taken over by the Egyptian god Osiris and began to talk of ridding the world of all its evils. Sir Thomas decided his companion was suffering from the heat and would be better once they returned to the more temperate climes of Europe, but in Rome Dadd became convinced that the Pope was one of the evils of which he had a mission to purge the world and it was only the vigilance of the Vatican Guard that prevented him from carrying out his intention of assassinating His Holiness.

Back in Britain, friends at once recognised the change that had come over Dadd. His former good naturedness was gone and he was argumentative and ill-tempered. He shunned company and lived much of the time on a diet of eggs and beer, filling his room with the empty eggshells.

His father, too, was most concerned about the change he saw in his son. Not without difficulty, he persuaded Richard to see a doctor, who diagnosed a mental illness and recommended treatment in an asylum. But Robert would have none of that and he decided to try to persuade his son to return home to live with him.

Richard refused but eventually suggested that he and his father might spend a little time together, just the two of them. They might return to Kent, he suggested, and visit Cobham, which they both remembered from their days at Chatham.

Robert agreed. He thought it would be a good opportunity to try again to talk his son into rejoining the family, where he could be looked after and perhaps made well again.

So the visit was arranged to coincide with the military display at Chatham, which they planned to watch together.

In fact, though, before they reached Chatham, Robert Dadd was murdered and his son Richard was nowhere to be found.

The handbill published by his family read as follows:
'MURDER! Missing, a young man about 24 years of age, labouring under insanity, and named Richard Dadd. He is the son of a gentleman, Mr Robert Dadd, who was cruelly murdered in Cobham Park, near the village of Cobham in Kent, on the evening of Monday, the 28th of August, 1843.

'The son accompanied his father from London to Gravesend and thence to the Ship Inn at Cobham on Monday afternoon; whence they went out for a walk together about half-past nine o'clock intending to return and sleep.

'The following morning, the body of the father was discovered, barbarously murdered, and lying beside it were found a stiletto knife and black handled razor, both of which appeared to be perfectly new – the name on the razor is Mosely and Co, New Street. The son has not since been heard of, whereby the anxiety of his friends is greatly increased, fearing he, too, may have met with the same fate as his unfortunate parent.

'The young man stands about 5 ft 8½ inches high, has dark hair, a scar on the forehead, light blue eyes, heavy dark eyebrows, without whiskers and is 21 years of age; his manner is reserved and sullen, he has a hurried gait and the appearance incident to persons labouring under a loss of intellect; had on a brown taglioni loose coat over a dark frock coat, buttoned up to the chin and sky blue cloth trousers.

'Any person finding or securing the said Richard Dadd shall receive a reward of £10 by applying to Mr C. Martin, 24 High Street, Strood, Kent.'

But before the notice was even printed, Richard was out of the country. He had gone from Cobham Woods to the Crown inn at Rochester, where he washed the blood off his hands and then ordered a post chaise to take him to Sittingbourne.

From there he went to Dover where he hired a boat and crossed to France, where he might well have remained if he had not attacked another passenger in a coach near Fontainbleu. He decided the other man was the Devil in disguise and tried to kill him. This time, however, he failed. He was arrested and committed to an asylum for the insane, from where he was collected some time later by English policemen who brought him back to the scene of his father's death.

There, after a very public and at times almost farcical trial, the Rochester magistrates committed him for trial at Maidstone Assizes.

In fact, though, he was never tried. Instead, he was certified under the Criminal Lunatic Act and committed to Bethlem (Bed-

The Fairy Feller's Master Stroke, one of the surrealist-style pictures painted by Richard Dadd after he was committed to Broadmoor for killing his father at Cobham (Picture: Tate Gallery).

lam) Hospital on August 22, 1844. He spent most of his remaining life there, dying in Broadmoor in 1886 aged 68.

Thanks to some enlightened supervision, despite the fact that he continued to be prone to violent outbursts, he was permitted full use of materials and continued to paint. Some of his 'mad' paintings are today among his most valued works, changing hands for many thousands of pounds each. In 1974 there was a special exhibition of his work at the Tate Gallery in London.

As he aged he became more and more withdrawn, but he had moments of real brilliance and some of his work included humorous cartoons and comic drawings. He also decorated the asylum theatre.

He was buried in the grounds of Broadmoor Hospital, leaving an artistic legacy that was remarkable for its allegorical and surrealistic quality. He had a sister who was also mentally ill so it may be that the defect was inherited.

If he had not been afflicted as he was, he might have become an even greater painter. Instead, he was doomed to be better known as the madman who murdered his own father in Cobham Woods.

THE SOLDIER'S
FAREWELL

DEDEA Redanies was a 26 year old soldier, of fair complexion and a little under average height. He was a pleasant looking young man; quiet, kindly, a Serb by birth. He had lived a fairly adventurous life before he joined the British Swiss Legion and was stationed at Shorncliffe, near Folkestone.

Born in 1830 the son of a minor civil servant, he was brought up under Turkish rule as a Moslem, but early in life he decided he wanted to travel and he accompanied his father to Egypt and other neighbouring countries.

Later, he enlisted in a cavalry regiment of the Austro-Hungarian Army and saw action at the battle of Szegadin, seat of the Hungarian Revolutionary Government, where he actually had his horse shot from under him. He was wounded twice and was taken prisoner, but when the Austrians offered to take him into their army he lost no time in joining the Reuss Regiment of cavalry and with that he fought at the battle of Novara in Italy in March 1849, which ended the revolution in Italy. He was again slightly wounded there.

Before the battle he had demonstrated his loyalty to his new masters by going disguised as a seller of spirits into the enemy camp where he got one of the men in charge of the colours drunk and, overpowering another man, stole the colours. Although he was fired upon, he managed to escape and swim back across the river that separated the two armies, still with the captured flag. For that exploit, he was awarded a gold medal and, later, he won another one.

His mercenary life continued and he was stationed for a while in Milan where he was converted to Christianity by a Capuchin monk, a fellow Serb, with whom he became friendly, and was baptised into the church.

Then, learning of the formation of the British Foreign Legions, he deserted from the Italian Army and, travelling by way of Sardinia to Switzerland, he enlisted.

Which was how he came to be stationed at Shorncliffe, in Kent, in 1855.

Because he was able to speak Italian and German as well as some English, he was appointed interpreter at the hospital at Dover castle. It was a fairly undemanding job that gave him plenty of spare time and excused him from much of the normal Army discipline. Like many of the soldiers stationed at Dover, he spent many an evening in the town and it was there, outside a theatre one evening, that he met two sisters, Caroline and Maria Back.

Caroline was 18 and her sister, Maria, 16 and both had something of a reputation for a fondness for the company of soldiers. They had plenty of opportunities to indulge it, for their mother, Mrs Mary Back, took in officers' washing. It wasn't long before Dedea was carrying laundry to and from the Back home, walking from Shorncliffe Camp through Folkestone to Dover, a distance of about eight or nine miles along the cliff tops.

After about a year, the young soldier was a frequent and welcome visitor to the house in Albion Place, Dover. Although he was very friendly with all the family, including Maria (who he called Mary Ann) it was Caroline with whom he had fallen in love and her parents, John and Mary Back, regarded him as her fiancee.

The relationship, however, seems not to have been an exclusive one. One evening, while Dedea was sitting with Caroline in the house, he saw an artilleryman come down the stairs. He was not unduly worried about it. Dedea was an easy-going, good humoured sort of chap and when, soon afterwards, he was sent to Aldershot for a time, he wrote several times to Caroline.

When he returned, he resumed his visits to her home and during one of these visits he asked her to show him the letters he had written to her, which she did.

But as well as his letters, she brought him, apparently by

mistake, another letter: one which greeted her 'My dear Caroline . . .' and looked forward to meeting her again when she came to Woolwich.

What else that letter contained, Dedea never knew because as soon as she realised her mistake, Caroline snatched it from him and threw it into the fire.

Even that did not change the young foreigner's feelings for his English girlfriend. On Saturday, August 2, 1856, he was again at the house in Albion Place where Caroline handed back to him a small portrait he had given her, saying that she was going away to visit her married sister Mary, in Woolwich.

Remembering the letter he had seen by mistake, Dedea feared that she was also going to meet the mysterious artilleryman and that he was losing her to his rival.

In an uncharacteristic fit of jealousy, he smashed the little portrait and threw it on to the fire, saying it was too small anyway and that he would get her a larger one that she could hang on her wall.

He left the house then and, at about 6pm, he went into the shop of a cutler named John Green in Dover and bought a poniard, a kind of flick knife, before returning to the Back's house in Albion Place, where he arrived at about 7.30pm.

He asked Caroline to walk back with him to Folkestone, to meet his sister who, he said, had travelled from Aldershot to see him and wanted to meet her future sister-in-law.

Mrs Back objected to that idea. She told Dedea she had taken Caroline to see a doctor who had told her she must rest as much as possible. She suggested they might travel to Folkestone by train, but Dedea swept aside such objections, saying a walk in the sunshine would do Caroline good.

It wasn't a question of money for the fare, he emphasised. His sister had brought him money and he had, in fact, £100.

In the end, Mrs Back allowed herself to be persuaded to permit Caroline to go with Dedea next morning, as long as they were chaperoned by Maria.

That was not what Dedea wanted, but it was the best he could get and in the end he agreed to it.

Quite how Redanies spent that Saturday night is in doubt. He himself said he spent it in the Back's house. Both John and Mary Back afterwards declared he did no such thing – but then, of course, to misquote a witness in a much later and more celebrated case, they would, wouldn't they?

They claimed Redanies left the house and slept they knew not where, returning at about 2am in order to collect the girls for an early start on the long walk to Folkestone.

Whichever was the truth – and the somewhat negative evidence available suggests that, in fact, the young soldier probably did spend the night in the house – John Back got up at the same time as his two young daughters on the Sunday morning and had breakfast with them and Redanies before he saw them off at about 3.30am, Redanies resplendent in his uniform red jacket and cap and the girls in light frocks with white stockings and short black capes round their shoulders.

It was the last time John Back saw his two daughters alive.

The three young people were all in high spirits, chattering and laughing together, when they were seen walking arm in arm, all three, at about 5am as they neared Folkestone.

Two hours later, a man called Thomas Gurling stopped at a public house called the Valiant Sailor, near the top of the hill leading out of Folkestone going towards Dover, to tell the landlord Richard Kitham that murder had been done on the cliff tops overlooking the town at a place known locally as Steddy Hole.

Kitham went to the place and there he found the bodies of two young girls. The two bodies were some little distance apart, the eldest girl nearest Folkestone. Both had been stabbed several times.

The bodies were taken immediately to a nearby house and, later that day, Mrs Back was brought there to identify her two daughters, Maria and Caroline.

As soon as the bodies were found, a hue and cry was raised but it was not until the following day, Monday, August 4, that Dedea Redanies was traced to the village of Lower Hardres, some three miles on the Folkestone side of Canterbury and about 20 miles from where the bodies were found.

There, inquiries discovered, he had bought some writing paper, envelopes and a pen from a grocer's shop owned by Mrs Elizabeth

Attwood and there, too, he had sat down to write two letters. Both were written in German: one addressed to Miss Caroline Back, 5 Albion Place, Dover and the other to Lieutenant Schmidt, the officer commanding the company with which Redanies served.

The fugitive then went to the village post office, where he bought two postage stamps and posted the letters. They were still in the post box when Police Superintendent William Walker arrived there with a magistrates' order for them to be handed over to him.

At about 4pm Redanies was spotted by an alert Constable Fryer about a mile from Canterbury. At that time he was without his uniform jacket and he wore a short black cape over his shoulders and another round his waist, where it looked rather like a skirt. With the help of some labourers, Fryer arrested the soldier and took him into custody.

It was not an entirely bloodless coup for the policeman, however. In an attempt to escape justice, Redanies stabbed himself several times with the poniard before it could be taken away from him, inflicting such wounds that he had to be taken to hospital where he remained for some time, not expected, at first, to live.

The dagger that produced the self-inflicted wounds was identified by a surgeon as probably the same one that killed Maria Back.

Dedea Redanies was duly brought to trial at the Winter Assizes in Maidstone in December 1856, where the letters he had written from Lower Hardres were read in court.

There was some doubt about the translation of some of the words and there were, in fact, two translations, in which some of the interpretations differed, giving slightly different meanings to some of the explanations given by the young soldier for his actions.

One letter was addressed to 'Dearest Mother Back'. In it, Dedea begged her forgiveness for the 'awful accident to the unlucky Dedea Redanies which I committed upon my very dear Caroline and Maria Back yesterday morning at five o'clock.'

He went on to explain that he had learned Caroline was not pregnant, after she had told him she was, and that she intended to go to Woolwich.

His letter explained: 'Because I cannot stay with my very dear

The Valiant Sailor inn today. Behind the inn is Steddy Hole, where the bodies of Caroline and Maria Back were found.

Caroline, it made my heart so scattered that I put into my mind at last that Caroline rather may die from my hands than allow Caroline's love being bestowed upon others.'

But, he went on, he had not intended to murder Mary Ann, her sister. She was in his way and so he had to stab her, too.

He declared he had no intention of committing this crime when he came to the house on Saturday evening, but when Caroline returned his picture and told him she was leaving, he went into the cutler's shop and bought the poniard with which to kill her.

He told in detail how, arm in arm, he had taken the two girls off the road and suggested that they all sit down. The girls had refused to do so because the grass was wet, so he told Caroline to walk on while he went behind Mary Ann and plunged the dagger into her heart. She dropped down with a dull cry and he at once rushed after Caroline.

He said she cried out: 'Dear Dedea!' and fell down, weeping, at which he rushed to her and gave her a last kiss 'as an everlasting remembrance'.

He then took the black capes from both girls and left the awful spot 'with weeping eyes and a broken heart'.

Redanies pleaded guilty to murdering Caroline but not Maria and his defence lawyer pleaded that he was, at the time, in such a state of mind that he was not able to judge the nature and quality of the act, as witness the incoherence of the letters and the fact that he was finally caught wandering about the countryside wearing the shawls of the two victims.

The jury took barely two minutes to reach a verdict of wilful murder and the black cap was duly donned.

Pronouncing sentence, the judge said he had no doubt the verdict was a proper one.

He went on: 'Your offence is not as hateful as though it had proceeded from the motive of obtaining the property of another; or of revenge, or any other motive hateful or detestable in itself. But you have allowed an ill-regulated passion to get the mastery over you and your conduct is, in reality, as selfish and as wicked as if it proceeded from any of the motives I have mentioned.

'Although, therefore, one may pity you more, it is necessary to make an example as much in this as in any other case of murder.'

The sentence of death was interpreted clause by clause to Redanies, who was reported to seem quite unmoved. When it was over, he walked coolly from the dock.

The execution of Dedea Redanies was the first to take place in Maidstone for seven years. While he was in prison awaiting execution, Redanies asked to see relatives of the two dead girls and Mrs Back travelled up from Dover to see him. He greeted her fondly, kissed her and begged her forgiveness, which she eventually granted.

It seems that throughout his imprisonment and trial he clung to a conviction that he had not so much murdered the sisters as despatched them to heaven before him, where Caroline, at least, would be (as it were) in safekeeping until he joined her again.

In conversation with a Roman Catholic priest, Fr Lawrence, who attended him in his cell, Redanies seems to have persuaded the priest that he was not sane. That view was expressed to the prison governor who advised that the Secretary of State should be informed at once. Fr Lawrence did in fact write to Home Secretary

Sir George Grey but on the very morning of the execution on January 1, 1857, a letter arrived from Whitehall saying that Sir George regretted he could discover no sufficient grounds to justify him in interfering with the due course of the law in this case. He did not doubt that the prisoner was not insane when he committed the murders but was fully responsible for his acts.

It was not until the night before his execution that Redanies expressed any regret for the crime he had committed.

One of his last acts was to hand to the priest another letter, written in German, for Mr and Mrs Back, to be given to them after he was dead. In it, he urged: 'Dear parents, Forget your anger against me and do not curse me in my grave. Remember that by doing so you would not only afflict me but also my dear Caroline and Maria. They love me as I love them. We are above with our Father again together, where we shall see one another again and live for ever with the Father of love, Jesus Christ.

'I greet you, with my dear Caroline and Maria, and wish you the blessings of God and prosperity until the voice of God calls you, too, to life everlasting.'

The letter was signed Caroline Back, Dedea Redanies, Maria Back.

On his last morning, after a disturbed night – the first, apparently, since his arrest – he was up at his usual hour and took special care to dress carefully, even though he had, of course, exchanged his uniform for prison dress.

He attended morning service in the prison chapel at 8.45 and returned to his cell where the executioner, Calcraft, came for him. He at once sprang to attention, allowed himself to be pinioned and was led out to the prison porter's lodge, where the scaffold had been erected. He took his place in the sombre procession to the gallows, marching resolutely and apparently almost cheerfully.

Right up to moments before his death, Redanies was still telling fellow prisoners that he would soon again see his dear Caroline and Maria, declaring: 'In a few moments I shall be in the arms of my dear Caroline – I care not for death!'

The execution was watched by between 4,000 and 5,000 spectators but there was none of the rowdiness that was a feature of so many public executions of the time and the police afterwards reported that not one single complaint of robbery had been reported to them during the incident.

In a bizarre way, Dedea Redanies, double murderer, became responsible for yet another death after his own execution.

Two men who were dismantling the gallows after the body had been removed, pulled away the heavy cross beams. One came away more easily than either of the men expected and one of the two, James Anderson, lost his balance and fell some 15ft to the ground.

He was rushed to a chemist's shop opposite the gaol but was found to be dead when he reached there.

POOR
FANNY WALLACE

FRANCES Wallace was a model mother. Everyone who knew her said so. But the daughter she loved and cared for so well was the living evidence of a secret poor Frances could not bear to think might be revealed. Rather than risk that secret being known, she killed her child and at once gave herself up.

Frances was a laundress in Dover. She was, by all accounts, a hard-working, church-going, young unmarried mother, whose child was in fact the illegitimate daughter of her sister's husband, although her sister did not know that.

There seemed to be no particular danger that the sister ever would know – until Frances met and became friendly with a young man named Bligh who lodged next door, in Town Wall Lane, at Dover.

No doubt she thought she could trust him with her secret. Perhaps her guilt weighed heavily upon her and she longed for someone to share it with her. But she made a mistake when she confided in her gentleman friend, Mr Bligh, because from the time she told him she became persuaded – rightly or wrongly – that he would not keep it to himself, but would tell her sister, who lived in London.

That was something she could not bear.

It seems there was some justification for her fears, because Bligh did, in fact, tell his landlord, Mr Wells, the story. Wells, a Scot, apparently persuaded Bligh that he should, indeed, go to Frances' sister and tell her the truth about the child's parentage.

At this time, Frances was ill and was convinced that she did not have long to live. The thought that she might die and leave her daughter to bear the brunt of her own wrong-doing, drove the young mother to the brink of insanity.

It was soon after 7am on Sunday, October 26, 1856 that the entire Town Wall Lane neighbourhood was alarmed by Frances Wallace's screams. Neighbours who rushed to the house, found her trembling uncontrollably and obviously extremely distressed. When they asked her what was the matter, she told them she had murdered her child and that the body was lying on the floor, inside the house.

One of her hands was covered in blood and when one of her friends, Elizabeth Mitchell, asked her what she had done to it she replied: 'I have been and murdered my own child – go in and look.'

The other woman went inside the house and there she found the tiny body lying on the floor opposite the fireplace in a pool of blood. The child's throat had been cut so savagely that the head was almost completely severed and there was a kitchen knife lying near the body, also covered in blood.

Horrified, the neighbour asked: 'How came you to do it?', to which Frances replied: 'It was through Mr Wells.'

She explained that Mr Wells had sent her man, Mr Bligh, away to her sister's by the six o'clock train.

The other woman's husband, John Mitchell, came and held Frances while his wife went to the police station. While they waited for a policeman to arrive, John asked Frances why she had killed her daughter, but all she could say was: 'That man!'

The policeman who arrived was a PC Irons, who found Frances and another woman in the room with the murdered child.

When he asked: 'Who did this?' Frances held out her hands, both now covered in blood, and said: 'Oh, policeman, what a hardened wretch I am!'

It was an expression she used two or three times before she added: 'That innocent dear – that intelligent creature!'

She told the constable she had been very ill and would not live long and said she had killed the child so that she would not be a trouble to people, as she had been.

She was very anxious about the time at which the excursion

The new Maidstone prison, which received its first prisoners in March, 1819. Frances Wallace was taken here in 1856.

train left for London, asking repeatedly: 'Does it go at six?'

When the constable said he did not know what time it left, she said: 'If that man's gone to my sister's there will be murder upon murder – there will be double murder.'

Asked what man she meant, she explained: 'A Scotchman next door.'

The constable examined the knife that was lying near the body. He thought it had been recently sharpened.

Frances was taken to the police station where, cautioned by the superintendent, she answered simply: 'I am guilty.'

The crime excited a great deal of interest in Dover, where Frances Wallace was quite well known and the very nature of the case was, besides, one that aroused public interest. When Frances was duly brought up before the magistrates, the Dover police court was crowded.

She looked haggard and ill and much older than her years and the Bench ordered a chair to be brought for her. In fact, however,

she fainted before it arrived and she did not fully recover throughout the rest of the proceedings.

She was charged with wilful murder. Asked if she had anything
to say, she first asked for time to think. But then, after a short
pause, she said: 'I have nothing to say.'

Witnesses were called and the case was heard. All the witnesses
vouched for the prisoner's previous good character and said she
had always seemed to be very affectionate with her daughter.

Whenever the child was mentioned during the hearing, Frances
was almost completely overcome with grief. So affecting was her
behaviour, in fact, that the spectators and even the magistrates,
including the Mayor of Dover himself, were moved to tears more
than once.

When it was over, the mayor told her: 'It is my painful duty to
commit you to the next Assizes at Maidstone, to take your trial
for the wilful murder of your child.'

Frances was taken to Maidstone prison to await trial. Mean-
time, an inquest on the child was held and a verdict of wilful
murder was returned against her.

The trial at assizes took place in December. Frances was unable
to stand in the dock and she was allowed to sit, between two
women warders who, from time to time, gave her a restorative.

Elizabeth Mitchell, Frances' neighbour in Town Wall Lane at
Dover, told the court she had known Frances for three years. She
said she had seen the defendant leave her house at about 7.30 that
fateful Sunday morning and had noticed that her hand was
covered in blood. Mrs Mitchell thought she had cut herself and
asked her how she had come to cut herself so badly.

Frances, however, replied that she had killed her own daughter.
Mrs Mitchell said she went at once into the house where she saw,
in a downstairs room, the child lying with its head nearly severed
from the body.

PC Irons told how he had arrived at the house and gone inside
with Mrs Mitchell and found the child lying on the floor. He
produced as evidence a table knife covered with blood and said
that Frances had spoken repeatedly in the most affectionate terms
of her child.

Charlotte Barton was an old woman who lived in the same

house, as Frances' lodger. She said the child slept with Frances only on Saturday and Sunday nights. She knew Frances went to bed on the Saturday night before the murder at about 9.30pm, by which time the child was already in bed.

Early next morning, Frances came to Mrs Barton's room with a candle. She was in her night clothes and said she had been woken up by Mrs Barton's coughing. The next thing Mrs Barton knew was when she heard a scream from Frances Wallace.

She said the child – she referred to her as 'little Fanny' – was a very attractive child and her mother was very proud of her, spending her earnings in dressing the child respectably. But lately, she had been in very low spirits.

She also said that Bligh used to come to the house occasionally, but declared she never saw him upstairs with Frances Wallace.

Superintendent Coram told the court that after the murder the prisoner was 'frantic', and kept screaming: 'Telegraph! Telegraph!' When she was being taken to Maidstone gaol, she said she wanted her pocket at home to be looked after because it had sugar of lead in it.

That was all there was to the prosecution case. There was, after all, no denial from the prisoner that she had committed the crime and all the evidence there was spoke for itself.

Her defending lawyer, however, told the jury there was sufficient cause why they should not pronounce a verdict of wilful murder. In an eloquent speech he first hinted that his client might not be as sane as the rest of them and then developed his theme, making the point that it did not need medical evidence to help twelve sane jurymen to decide whether or not the circumstances of a case were consistent with sanity.

He told them: 'Twelve men of common sense, such as usually appear in the jury box, are fully capable of deciding on that point.'

He went on to ask 'What motive was there in this case?' He claimed the prosecution had shown no motive for wilful, malicious, deliberate murder and he argued that the frantic state in which the prisoner was found, the dishevelled manner in which her clothes were put on, the wandering about in the night with a candle, the wild character of the expressions she used and the fact of her having poison in her pocket, all went to prove insanity.

'If she had been intending a wilful and deliberate murder,' he said, 'would she not rather have used the poison and attempted to conceal the crime than have imbrued her hands in the blood of a child to which all the evidence went to show she was fondly attached?'

He concluded that there was no motive; that it was a murder against all human motive and he suggested that the feeling of a mother for a loved child was a passion which men could hardly understand.

Frances was given a character reference from a Dover clergyman, a Mr Robins, who said he had known her for three years. He knew the child was not born in wedlock and added: 'God forbid I should speak lightly of that sin, but as far as I have been able to ascertain from the time of the birth of the child, her conduct towards it has been most exemplary.

'She was a most industrious person, distinguished for her amiability and extremely beloved by all persons of her own class who were acquainted with her.

'The affection this poor woman bore to her child was something most unusual. It was almost unprecedented. I scarcely ever saw such a depth of tender affection as she had for her little child.

'She attended my church regularly. I have often seen her there. I have seen her at church with her child standing up by her side. It was not possible that there could be a greater outer appearance of deep affection for her child.

'I should have thought no person less capable of harming her child than poor Fanny Wallace.'

During his summing up, the judge was so affected that at one time he had to pause to wipe tears from his eyes, and there was hardly a dry eye in the court. In spite of his own emotional example though, he cautioned the jury against being carried away by their feelings and left it to them to say whether or not the learned counsel had made out the insanity of the prisoner.

It took the jury just five minutes to decide that he had, and they returned a verdict acquitting Frances Wallace of the wilful murder charge on the grounds of insanity.

THE JILTED SUITOR

STEPHEN Fox thought that life, which had not been terribly kind to him, had taken a turn for the better when he met Mary Ann Hadley.

He was a 22 year old carpenter's plane-maker then, originally from Dover although his parents had moved to Canterbury while he was still quite young. They had then separated, leaving him and his five siblings in their mother's care. She was not able to afford much in the way of schooling for any of them and Stephen had to start work when he was eight. By the time he was twelve he was a chair-maker, a trade he later abandoned in favour of plane-making.

A lively young man, inclined to be vain about his appearance, he was fond of places of public amusement, although he was never a great drinker and he never lost the chapel-going habit of his childhood.

By the time he was 18 he had fallen in love with a young woman who, however, broke off the relationship after a few months. Later though, she became his mother's domestic servant and the two became lovers as a result of which she bore him an illegitimate child.

When his mother died, the mother of his child left the house and Stephen turned his affections upon Mary Ann Hadley.

She, of course, knew nothing about the other woman or the baby. She lived with her parents, Edward and Harriet Hadley, in Coldharbour Lane, Canterbury and she worked as a part-time laundress in the house of a Mrs Carter near the barracks, in Sturry Road.

Although Mrs Hadley did not approve of him, Stephen and

Mary Ann had been walking out together for about two years in May 1857 and on Sunday, May 10, they went to chapel together, as usual, once in the morning and again in the evening, even though they had not been on such good terms lately as they had been before.

He dined at her house with her family and in the afternoon, he walked in the garden with her father.

But when he called at the house on Monday, her mother told him Mary Ann did not wish to see him, and that she was, in any case, not at home.

He went away, but he was back on Tuesday only to be told the same thing. Mary Ann was not at home and her mother did not know where she was. Again, he went away, but this time he came back later. Indeed, he returned several times before, at last, she came home at about 10.15pm.

They went into the front parlour together although Mrs Hadley was careful to leave the door ajar so that she could hear all that was said.

Mary Ann told Fox it was no good his coming to the house any more because she wanted no more to do with him. She had found out about the other woman and his child and although it was too delicate a matter for her to speak about to his face she said she had already written and posted a letter to him explaining her change of heart and he would get it in the morning.

Fox became very angry, demanding to be allowed to see her just one more time at least, but Mary Ann told him she had made inquiries and had learned that the rumours she had heard about him were true.

However, she did agree to meet him again at 8pm the next day but when he went to the house at 7pm, her mother told him she had been home and had gone out again.

Desperately, he went to Mrs Carter's house but no-one there knew where he might find Mary Ann. Back in Coldharbour Lane he called at the home of Edward Gurney, who lived opposite the Hadleys and was a friend of the family.

Mr Gurney was a gardener who knew Fox and in the course of their conversation Fox told him that Mary Ann had deceived him.

Gurney tried to jolly him out of his black mood.

'Pooh!' he said. 'There are plenty more girls besides her.'

But Fox would not be appeased.

'There are none I like as well as her,' he said. Then he added: 'Can you keep a secret?'

Gurney promised he could and Fox took a pistol from his pocket and showed it to Gurney.

'That shall be her doom tonight before I sleep!' he said. He took out four bullets, saying: 'One of these shall do it if the others don't.'

Gurney told him not to be silly, saying he'd be hung for it, but Fox replied he'd as soon be hung for her as not and Gurney decided the best thing he could do was to take Fox to a nearby pub, the Cambridge Arms, and calm him down with a drink or two.

However, Fox was not a drinking man and he wasn't in the mood for social drinking. While Gurney had a glass of porter, Fox settled for a ginger beer.

Later on that evening, Mrs Hadley came to the pub with her sister and spoke to Gurney, asking him if Fox was drunk. He assured her he was not, which was perfectly true. When Mrs Hadley went away again, Fox followed her.

'What's up, Mrs Hadley?' he demanded. 'I just want to see my Polly.'

Mrs Hadley told him her daughter did not want to see him again, but he swore he would see her once more, at any rate. Mrs Hadley, who now feared for her daughter's safety, told him Mary Ann was spending the night on the other side of town, although in fact she knew the girl was at home.

Fox became abusive and threatening and Mrs Hadley sought the help of a policeman to whom she complained of the man's behaviour. The policeman went to look for Fox, but he had disappeared.

That night, still concerned for Mary Ann's safety, after some of the things Fox had been saying, Gurney and Mrs Hadley arranged for the girl to sleep at the Gurney house instead of her own and next morning Mr Gurney went with her to her work in Sturry Road.

Their way took them past the barracks at about 6.50 on the

Wednesday morning, May 13, and there they found Fox waiting for them in a passageway with a pistol in each hand. He had been waiting there for at least an hour and as he stepped out to confront them he told Gurney to keep out of it or he would get shot as well.

Then almost immediately he fired both pistols. One of the bullets hit Mary Ann in the thigh, severing the femoral artery and causing such loss of blood that she died less then an hour later in the arms of a young man who happened to be passing at the time of the shooting and who carried her into Mrs Carter's house.

As soon as the pistols were discharged, Gurney tackled the gunman and wrested the weapons from him. Then he and another man took Fox to the police station, where he was searched and relieved of the pistols, a powder flask, some caps and four bullets.

At the police station Fox told PC James Epps: 'I had never had a cross word with her all the time we kept company.'

But he went on to say he had been deceived once and he did not mean to be deceived again. He also said it was a good thing the police had not interfered because he would have shot them or anyone else who got in the way.

Fox was duly charged with the wilful murder of Mary Ann Hadley and tried at Maidstone Assizes in August 1857.

At the trial, the letter which Mary Ann told him she had posted to him was read. In it, she said:

'Sir – Your conduct of late has been anything but what it should be when a young man considers himself engaged. You have always all along strongly denied having any connection with Miss B....., but I am sorry to say that I have, during the last week, been fully convinced that your statement is not a correct one and that you have to pay for its maintenance and, therefore, I think as such is the case, I had better at once break off the engagement. Yours etc.'

The letter was signed Mary Ann Hadley. There was a postscript which added: 'PS You can have your clothes and the things I have of yours on Saturday next.'

Also read in court was a statement which Fox made after his arrest on the day of the murder.

In that, he said: 'Of course, the reason why I did it was because she deceived me. I had promised her marriage, she consented.'

The statement went on to detail his movements while he was

trying to see Mary Ann at her home and ended: 'I did not see her last evening at all. She would not see me. I did not see her until seven o'clock this morning.

'She said: 'Stephen, forgive me' and I said: 'No, I can't.' I have nothing more to say.'

The letter was signed with a cross, his mark, for he could not write his own name.

Fox's defending counsel made the best of a bad job, inviting the jury to doubt whether the state of mind of the prisoner at the time the shots were fired made him responsible to the law for his deed.

He declared: 'Of all the passions which sway the human heart, none more utterly than disappointed love sway reason on her throne or lead to more tragical results.'

He said Fox had been the acknowledged suitor of the deceased. He went with her to chapel, visited her three or four times a week, and dined at her home.

But then, on Monday, he was denied access to her and his hopes of happiness were suddenly crushed. The result, said the lawyer, was a state of extraordinary excitement and, reminding the jury of a quotation: 'Anger is a short madness', he recommended the jury to give the safest verdict of not guilty on the grounds of insanity.

In his summing up, the judge pointed out that uncontrollable impulse was not an answer to a charge of murder. The prisoner's own statement before magistrates, on the very day the deed was done, was perfectly lucid and coherent and utterly irreconcilable with any theory of insanity.

The jury agreed with him. It took them no more than a few minutes to return a verdict of guilty.

The execution took place on Thursday, August 27, 1857. It was a double execution shared by Fox with the Maidstone fratricide, Edwards.

As the sombre procession left the gaol for the porter's lodge, outside of which the scaffold stood, Fox sang a hymn which he continued while the executioner, Calcraft, pinioned him and brought him to stand on the drop. He then had to wait for Edwards to be made ready also.

Moments later both were dead.

There was a sequel to the events in Maidstone that August morning, reported in *The Canterbury Observer* of August 22 under the heading: 'Service for Fox at St Margaret's Church'.

The report continued: 'We regret to find that the rumour with regard to this subject, to which we referred last week, is correct and that the service is to be held and the Communion administered this (Thursday) morning on behalf of the murderer Fox.

'We think nothing can be more ill-judged or uncalled for than this proceeding. From its very singularity the service will be sure to attract attention and will be the means of conferring a dangerous distinction upon the detestable crime for which Fox justly dies on the scaffold today.

'If the man had been executed here, as a few lovers of such scenes morbidly desired, there would have been some show of reason for such a service as an antidote to the harm which, to our mind, public executions frequently occasion.

'But the execution taking place at Maidstone, where can be the possible good of attempting to excite a spurious expression of public sympathy in Canterbury at the hour when the sentence of death is to be carried out?

'Far be it from us to defraud the wretched man of the shortest prayer of the humblest Christian house, but we repeat that devotions for such a purpose should be performed in private. A public act so singular as this service challenges criticism; and we unhesitatingly affirm that no possible public good can accrue from its performance.'

THE CAIN AND ABEL KILLER

NO fewer than five murderers were executed at Maidstone
in 1857 for crimes committed during the two years 1856
and 1857 and several more were tried who escaped the
death penalty for one reason or another.

This exceptional series of executions began on January 1 with
the judicial death of Dedea Redanies (see chapter four). But
George Edwards created a rather special stir in his home town
when he joined the infamous quintet in August that year. His
crime was one that has earned especial condemnation since
murder was first recorded.

The Edwards family lived at 21 Bedford Row, Maidstone, on
the Boxley Road not far from Maidstone prison. They were the
father and mother, Daniel and Mary Ann Edwards, and their three
sons, Thomas, 24, George, 18, and Samuel who was about nine
years old.

The family was in fact descended from a Welsh soldier who
came to Coxheath, just outside Maidstone, in 1793 as a paymaster
at the army camp there. In that role he saved enough money to buy
a farm which, when he died, was inherited by his son, Daniel.
Unfortunately, the son did not also inherit the father's business
acumen and he was soon in financial difficulties that eventually led
to his having to give up the farm and move into Maidstone, where
he became a day labourer.

The house in Bedford Row was an ordinary four-roomed house
with a cellar and one of the two bedrooms, in the front of the

A Maidstone street scene in the 1850s as George Edwards would have known it.

house, was shared by little Samuel with his parents while the back room was shared by Thomas and George.

The front door of the house opened directly on to the street and there was a small back kitchen which led into a yard and a brick-paved passage which ran along the backs of several of the houses. Stairs led up from the kitchen to the bedrooms and there was another flight of stairs down to the cellar.

Thomas Edwards was generally regarded as a steady, well-behaved and hardworking young man, but his brother George was very different. He was a loner, who would disappear into the cellar if his mother had callers at the house while he was there. One of his eccentricities was his habit of going to the cellar and lathering his face and shaving himself with a razor, sometimes for an hour at a time.

He only ever left the house at night but although he kept bad company he was not in the habit of getting drunk and he was said to be fond of flowers and animals. His last work had been looking after farm animals and he was particularly fond of the family cat.

His father worried about his son's disinclination to work and tried to find employment for him. On Saturday, March 17, 1857, when George had not had a proper job for about 18 months, Mr Edwards came home from work and told George he had found work for him with his own employer.

George at once said he didn't need a job. He said he already had one somewhere else. This was clearly not true and there was a family quarrel during which Thomas, his brother, threatened to turn him out of the house if he did not go to work.

However, come bedtime the two brothers went to their shared room, the quarrel apparently over at least for the time being.

Two days later on Monday evening, both parents, Thomas and little Samuel were all at home. George, as usual in the evening, was out. Thomas went to bed at about 8.30 and his father and Samuel went up at about 9.30, leaving Mrs Edwards downstairs on her own, waiting for George to come home.

While she waited, she got on with a few chores, including going down into the cellar to chop wood for the fire in the morning. She used an axe which, when she had finished, she left in the cellar.

George returned home at about 9.30 and his mother finally went to bed at about 10.15, leaving George sitting downstairs in the back room on his own.

Thomas was fast asleep by this time and some ten minutes after she went up his mother heard her other son, George, coming up to the room. Because of George's habit of going out during the night, she went back downstairs to make sure he had not left any of the doors unlocked. Satisfied that all was secure, she returned to her room and went to bed. Very soon she too was asleep.

A couple of hours later though, Mr Edwards was awakened by a noise in the back bedroom of their house. He woke his wife and by candlelight they went together to the boys' room. There they found a candle burning and Thomas was lying on his bed in a welter of his own blood.

Appalled by what he found, Mr Edwards rapped on the partition wall that separated him from his neighbours, the King family, at No 20. There, 13 year old Frances King was already awake, having been disturbed by what she later described as a chopping noise in the back bedroom of the Edwards' house. She heard a window opening and someone run along the passageway that connected the backs of the row of houses. Frightened, she called her mother and when they heard Mr Edwards rapping on the wall, she went next door with her father.

In fact, however, it was not the Kings who were first to arrive on the scene, but the Edwards' neighbour on the other side, Mr Lee. They found the window of the room the two Edwards brothers shared was open and flowerpots which had been on the window sill lay smashed on the ground below. A pane of glass was broken in the window below too, apparently by someone's foot as he climbed out of the upper window.

The police were called and an axe was found under the bed in which Thomas Edwards lay, not yet dead but deeply unconscious. It was the same axe that Mrs Edwards had earlier used to chop firewood in the cellar. Now it was covered in blood and human hair.

Thomas Edwards' head had been viciously hacked and there were four severe axe wounds. He died at about 8am, without regaining consciousness.

George Edwards was nowhere to be found and the inescapable conclusion to be drawn was that he had murdered his brother with the axe and then escaped through the window.

In fact, he had gone to his uncle, another Thomas Edwards, who lived at Brompton, near Chatham, arriving there at about 9am the next day. This Mr Edwards was a Royal Marine pensioner and he had not seen his nephew for some years. When he arrived at the house, George had to explain who he was. He said he had been up all night after taking a young woman home to Boxley, a village between Maidstone and Chatham.

The uncle gave him some breakfast and they had a pint of beer together and then, when George said he felt sleepy, his uncle told him to take off his coat and boots and lie down on his bed for a while.

It was quite a while; George didn't wake up until 5pm, when the two men had tea together and George stayed there until 9pm when he suggested that they should go back to Maidstone together. The older man said he didn't think he would. It was too late, he said.

So George said in that case he would go into Rochester to see someone. If he didn't return to Maidstone that night, he said, he would come back to the house next morning.

Then he left, but he did not return.

On Tuesday, March 20, PC Thomas Smith of the City of Rochester police, having heard of the murder in Maidstone, was keeping an eye open for anyone of George Edwards' description. When he saw him in Rochester High Street going towards Gravesend at 5am, he approached him and clapped a hand on his shoulder.

'Edwards?' he asked. Edwards made no attempt to deny it. He said he had left Maidstone the night before last, but he refused to say where he had slept the previous night.

Told he was being taken into custody for misusing his brother Thomas (the constable did not yet know that Thomas had since died), George replied: 'Not me!'

Nevertheless, he was taken to the police station where he was put in one of the cells. He was told to take off his coat, but he didn't want to, declaring: 'You'll find no spots of blood on me!'

Although he was searched, in fact no spots of blood were found on him and when he was being charged with chopping his brother with an axe he again replied: 'Not me!'

In due course, the case came to trial at Kent Assizes in August 1857. His defence lawyers wanted him to plead insanity. George's general demeanour and behaviour might well have justified such a plea but Edwards himself would not agree to that. Instead, he insisted he was innocent of the crime of which he was accused.

His lawyer did his best. The whole evidence against the prisoner, he argued, was purely circumstantial. He reminded the jury that although it was evident that the doors of the Edwards house on the fatal night had been fastened, the windows, back and front, were not. The prisoner was known to be of eccentric nocturnal habit. Was it all that improbable, he asked, that he had left the house and that some midnight marauder had got in and attacked the first person who discovered him?

It was not a very convincing scenario and the judge, for one, was not persuaded by it. In his summing up, he said in all his experience he had never heard a defence of that kind put forward upon so little evidence.

The poverty of the Edwards household and its position were wholly inconsistent with the idea of a desperado going in to rob and murder. Besides, no robbery had in fact taken place and any such supposed desperado must have first searched for the axe, found it in the cellar and then taken it upstairs where the murder was committed.

The jury retired to consider their verdict at 2.25pm. It took them about ten minutes to decide that George Edwards was guilty.

Hearing their verdict, Edwards murmured: 'Thank God, I am innocent for all that.'

Sentence of death was passed and Edwards was led away.

Right up to the day before his execution, Edwards protested his innocence, although several times he referred to his brother's death, saying: 'It served him right.'

Finally, on his last night, he bowed to pressure from the Rev Joseph Knott and wrote a statement which he declared was the whole truth.

He said that on the night of the murder he had walked into the town and met a young woman he knew. He went with her to Boxley and back to Maidstone again and stayed with her until about midnight. Then he went home to go to bed.

He went on: 'I pulled off my jacket and was going to undress and get into bed when the deceased said he should lock me out another night if I came in so late. He said he was a good mind to do it that night.

'I being under the influence of liquor, high words began to rise between us. There was a lot of walking sticks in the corner of the room. He took one of them up and struck me with it on the head.

'It happened to hit the bedpost before it hit my head and that made it come on my head all the lighter. If it had happened to hit me first on the head, it would have killed me on the spot. If I had not bobbed on one side when he struck that blow it would have been fatal.

'I being so excited at the time I ran downstairs and got the axe and went upstairs again. Just as I got up top of the stairs he struck me with the stick. It hit me on the arm where I carried the marks several days.

'As he struck me with the stick, I ran in at him with the axe and then we had a regular duel. He fell backwards on the bed – that is when I struck the blows. After that, I put the axe under the bed and opened the window and throwed my jacket out. That knocked the flowerpots out of the window. One of them bounced and hit the window and broke one of the panes.

'So I can assure you it was done in great excitement and irritation.

'Then I left the house and went down town and stopped in a brothel till about three o'clock in the morning. Then I started off and went to Chatham.

'If he had not spoke to me the night in question, I being under the influence of liquor that my temper rose all the quicker, I should not have committed that atrocious, horrible and diabolical deed. Though I struck so hard at the deceased, I never had no intention of doing what I did. However, it is done now and I am very sorry for what I have done. I hope he is now in Paradise – that is all the harm I wish him.'

Edwards also wrote a number of other letters, including one to his parents and one to the young woman with whom he said he spent the rest of the night after he had murdered his brother.

That letter he sent under cover of one to the Rev Joseph Knott, asking that it be sent to *Reynolds News* to make sure it was seen by the lady in question. In fact, it was also shown to the local newspaper.

In it, Edwards wrote: 'This sad occurrence has turned out very bad for me; worse than what you thought it would, my dear. Never mind, bear it patiently. I hope we shall have the pleasure of being together in the eternal world. A few more hours then I shall be launched into eternity.

'So, farewell my beloved pet, from your sincerely affectionate and loving, George Edwards.'

That morning, Edwards was visited by a young woman who said she was his cousin but who was almost certainly the one to whom he had written. His youngest brother was also brought to see him.

There was a last minute attempt to get his sentence commuted. A petition ('not numerously signed') was sent to Home Secretary Sir George Grey, pleading that the evidence against Edwards was entirely circumstantial and pointing out that the accused still persisted in declaring his innocence.

But Sir George replied that he could see no grounds for doubting the correctness of the verdict or anything that would justify him in advising any interference with the due course of law.

George Edwards was executed at Maidstone on August 27, 1857. He was the first person to be executed for fratricide at Maidstone for 200 years – coincidentally almost on the exact anniversary of that occasion when, on August 21, 1655, Freeman Sonds, second son of Sir George Sonds of Lees Court, Faversham, was executed on Penenden Heath for the murder of his eldest brother.

After the execution, the Rev Mr Knott was accused by the owner of *Reynolds News* of failing to fulfil his promise to the dead man to deliver the letter to the newspaper. The accusation prompted Mr Knott to write to *The Maidstone Journal* and *Kentish Advertiser* denying that he had made any such promise.

In his published letter, he said Edwards had given him three letters, all in one bundle. They were not addressed and Mr Knott had to read them to know for whom each was intended.

Two of the letters he duly delivered, but he said the one intended for the newspaper contained only 'a mass of licentious gossip about a number of women of the town.'

He added: 'I considered the interests of public decency and morality would not be furthered by its publication and so I kept it.'

He did not say he destroyed it and it could be that it has survived to be discovered by some diligent (and lucky!) researcher at some time.

MURDER
ON THE LINES

A T about 5.30pm on July 23, 1862 the body of a young boy was found behind a heap of chalk on Chatham Lines at Gillingham, beginning a sequence of events that ended with the execution of a young man who was, indeed, eccentric if not something more than that.

Robert Alexander Burton was born in Chatham in 1844. His father was a dockyard labourer and he himself was the youngest of the family. He was spoilt, particularly by his mother, and he grew up with a craving for notoriety. He made friends with undesirable characters and was a leader in mischief while playing truant from school.

When he left school at the age of 14, his father apprenticed him to Chatham builder and surveyor John Andrews but apprenticeship became so burdensome that young Robert ran away. For that he was taken to court, where he promised not to repeat the offence and was taken back.

In 1861, however, he did run away again. He pawned the valuable tools his father had given him and with the money he went to Portsmouth to try to join the Royal Navy. On that occasion, friends wrote to the authorities and he was prevented from going to sea.

While he was in Portsmouth, however, he got into trouble when he ordered a meal costing 2s 6d (12½p) and instead of paying for it he hit the waiter, knocking him to the ground, and then threw a pickle jar at him before he ran off.

He came back to Chatham, but his father refused to have him

in the house and his employer would not take him back this time. He was forced to make what money he could by doing occasional odd jobs where and when he could.

He next joined the militia in Maidstone and after serving a month he received his bounty money and returned to Chatham, making straight for a local brothel where he spent most of his money and was robbed of the rest.

He spent two months doing hard labour in prison at Canterbury for robbing Mr Clarke, a local shoemaker for whom he did some work. He blamed Mr Clarke for sending him to prison and when he was sentenced he told the magistrates: 'You may do as you like with me, but as for Clarke, I will give him something when I come out.'

The tragic events of that day in July 1862 began, ordinarily enough, at about 1pm when a nine year old boy, Thomas Houghton, was with his mother in Chatham.

They saw a baker's boy, William Clift, wheeling his barrow in Cage Lane. The boy's nose was bleeding and Mrs Houghton showed some concern, saying her own little boy's nose sometimes bled and she had great difficulty in stopping it.

The Houghtons knew Clift because he delivered bread to their house and he knew little Tommy well: a quiet, good-tempered and inoffensive lad.

The little exchange was overheard by a young man who stood nearby. He was Robert Burton, a lively, cheeky-looking 18 year old now, who told the baker's boy he had been shopping for a penny loaf but had been unable to get one at the shop lower down the street.

'Do you have one?' he asked. Clift, however, did not have one, so Burton walked with the baker's boy up the hill towards another baker's shop, owned by Mr Nicholson.

The Houghton boy walked with them a little way, he on one side of the barrow and Burton on the other, until Burton volunteered to push the barrow while Clift mopped his bleeding nose.

At Mr Nicholson's shop, Burton bought his penny loaf and turned back down the hill, following the younger boy back towards Cage Lane. But little Tommy Houghton did not go home. Instead, he went off to play on The Lines, a recreational area of open land that was originally part of the Napoleonic landward defences of Chatham Dockyard.

Burton also went up on to The Lines, where he saw the boy again.

There were no witnesses to exactly what happened next, but at about 5.30 that evening another boy, Albert Tree, was playing hare and hounds with some of his friends when he went behind a chalk heap to hide. There he saw a boy lying on the ground, dead, and at once he ran to two men who were walking nearby. One of them was Thomas Everist, who was crossing The Lines from New Brompton station.

'Hey mister, there's a boy been murdered behind that chalk heap,' gasped young Albert.

Everist wasn't sure, at first, whether to believe him or not, but he was persuaded to make the short diversion to the chalk heap and see for himself. What he saw persuaded him that murder had, in fact, been done there and the other man hurried off to fetch a policeman while Everist stayed beside the lifeless little body.

Eventually, Chatham's Police Sergeant Fisher arrived on the scene. News of the killing had spread and a little crowd of ghoulish townsfolk was already streaming towards the chalk heap on The Lines. Among them was George Houghton, little Tommy's brother. Another who hurried to the scene, summoned by the police, was local surgeon George Lock.

They found the body lying on its back, arms bent. The throat had been cut, the face and arms were covered in blood and there were bruises on both sides of the face, too. The boy's waistcoat and jacket were bloody and the shirt was hanging out and covered in blood. His braces were unbuttoned from the trousers and only one button of the waistband was fastened. About seven ft from the head there was a pool of blood and some four ft in the opposite direction was another pool of blood.

Mr Lock judged the boy had been dead about four hours by the time he saw the body. It was then 6.30pm, making the time of death about 2.30pm.

The body was taken to a nearby public house, the Napier Arms, and a post mortem examination next day revealed that the throat wound was the fatal one, although discolouration of the throat suggested the boy had also been partly strangled with his own necktie.

At this point there was no direct evidence to identify the killer, but as it happened that proved to be no great hindrance to police investigations for later that night, between 11 and 12, Burton came to the stables which the Chatham police rented for the county horses and told PC Stanley Hibberd: 'It was me who murdered that boy on The Lines today.'

The constable looked at Burton and saw a young man dressed untidily in dirty clothes, his sleeves tucked up.

'Did you, now?' he said and, without any difficulty being caused by Burton, he took him straight to the home of Supt Everist, who lived only four doors away from the dead boy's mother.

When he saw where they were heading, Burton's demeanour changed.

'Hey, you're not going to take me to the boy's mother, are you?' he asked. Told no, that was not where they were going, he relaxed again and became talkative, explaining just what had happened up there on The Lines earlier that day.

'I saw the boy go up to The Lines,' he said. 'I asked him to go behind the chalk pile. I hit him in the neck and threw him down and then grasped him by the neck and squeezed him until the blood gushed out of his nose and mouth. Then I tramped on his face.'

He gave all these details without any prompting or questioning by Hibberd. When they reached the Superintendent's house, Hibberd told his superior: 'This young man says he killed the boy on Chatham Lines.'

Everist cautioned Burton, who said: 'Well, I've made up my mind to tell you the truth and tell you all about it.'

He did so. At one point, Hibberd asked Everist: 'Which side did you say the boy was stabbed in the neck?' Everist replied: 'The left.'

But Burton burst in: 'No it is not, indeed, sir. If you look you'll find it's in the right – just here.' He pointed to his own neck and added: 'He struggled and fought very hard to the last. He caught hold of me several times about the arms and I dare say you will find some of his blood on my frock.'

Supt Everist examined him and, indeed, blood was found on the upper part of the sleeves. The lower part had been washed.

Burton went on: 'He caught hold of me once by the necktie – I don't know whether you'll find any blood on that or not.'

There was blood on it.

Burton said he had no particular ill-feeling against the boy but he had made up his mind to murder somebody. He said he knew the boy and his mother and knew where they lived.

He offered to show the Superintendent where the murder weapon was and together they walked to the back of a pub called The Dark Sun. There, directed by Burton, Everist reached up under the eaves and found the knife. As he inspected it by the light of a lantern, Burton told him: 'You needn't look for blood on it. I cleaned it by jobbing it into the ground.'

Next day, Burton was taken before magistrates who remanded him and while he was in custody, Burton told Supt Everist: 'I don't want to see the mother of the boy – that's the only thing that touches me. You see her and ask if she recollects being with the boy I killed at the bottom of Chatham about one o'clock that day. That's the first time I saw the boy that day. She'll recollect it if you ask her if she remembers a boy with a baker's barrow coming along with his nose bleeding. The mother spoke to the baker's boy and said her boy's nose often bled and she had a rare job to stop it.

'I was waiting for the baker's cart and I went on to Mr Nicholson's for a penny loaf. I got the loaf and the boy turned back. Afterwards, I went up on to The Lines, where I saw the little boy again.

'After I killed him, my hands were very wet with blood. I pulled the boy's shirt out and wiped my hands dry. I put the knife in my pocket where it wore a hole.

'Then I went across The Lines to the horse trough to wash my hands but I saw so many people about I went on to the soldiers' bathing pond. After I had washed my hands there, I crossed The Lines and went down through the Sally Port to Mr Discomb's, where I had a job of work carrying out stone.

'Mr Clarke may thank his stars he left Chatham, for he was the man I had made up my mind to murder. He was my ruin. He was the man that prosecuted me and I made up my mind to kill him when I came out of gaol.'

He said he would give no trouble. He would plead guilty, having made up his mind to murder someone because he was tired of life.

While on remand in Maidstone prison, Burton was at first very irritable and reckless but then he quietened and began to take an interest in religious matters. When he was transferred to another part of the prison, though, he again became very violent and refused to listen to any advice, threatening to destroy himself.

At his trial at Maidstone Assizes for the wilful murder of little Tommy Houghton, Burton at first pleaded guilty and treated the whole thing as an unnecessary formality. However, on the advice of the judge, he changed his plea to one of not guilty.

The defence called witnesses to try to show that Burton was of unsound mind when the murder was committed.

Chatham builder John Andrews, to whom Burton was once apprenticed as a carpenter, said the youngster was always very strange in his ways.

'There was always a vacant look about him,' he told the court. 'It was as if he was absorbed in thought. When he was set to work he would sometimes leave off and run about the yard and act very strangely, not seeming to know what he was about.

'This happened quite frequently and he was always looked upon as being of weak intellect.'

On one occasion, he was absent from work and when he returned, very dirty and red-faced, he said he had been to Canterbury to enlist and had run all the way back to Chatham.

He ran off again, more than once, and on one occasion went to Portsmouth to join the navy. Each time he returned after a few days.

One of Andrews' employees, Richard Evenden, said he had been deeply impressed by Burton's strange manner and eccentric habits. He could be extremely violent, he said, and recalled one occasion when Burton was found sitting in a coal cellar, looking very wild, with his eyes fixed on the ground. Asked what he was doing there, he rushed out of the door.

Another former employer, Philip Tillman, a Chatham grocer, said he had known Burton for five or six years and he had formerly been a shop boy in his employ, living in for just over a year. Mr

Tillman said he once found Burton in the cellar eating soap and on another occasion he was found eating a rushlight.

On yet another occasion, he said, he had seen Burton eating a cat which had been baked in a pie. The head was left lying in the yard and another man, Stephen French, said he saw a lad bring Burton a cat which he killed. He ate part of it and the rest was put into a pie and sent to the bakehouse to be cooked. When it was returned, Burton ate about threequarters of it and left the rest for his supper that night.

Mr French said that once, when he and Burton went together to the May Fair at Maidstone, Burton told him during the course of a conversation: 'In three months' time I shall be hung here on the gallows.'

The Burton family doctor, Dr Fayle, said he had sent Burton's mother to a lunatic asylum twice. Once she had tried to commit suicide. Burton also had a brother who, according to the doctor, was of unsound mind.

He told the court: 'I have given special attention to the study of insanity and I believe the prisoner labours under moral insanity but at the same time he knows perfectly well what he is about, although he has no control whatever over himself.

'It is an established fact that the intellect of a man may be vigorous and strong while his moral powers are altogether diseased. Moral disease of the brain is to be accounted for by some misconstruction of the organs. I believe a man could work out a proposition in Euclid and at the same time eat a cat.'

That caused some laughter in the court, but the point was made.

Burton's lawyer, in his closing speech, said his client had a vehement desire to be hanged and he argued that this was the strongest proof of his insanity.

But the prosecution pooh-poohed that argument, saying that if it were held that moral insanity excused the commission of a crime, then all criminals might be excused.

A medical witness for the prosecution, Edward Harold, said a person labouring under a strong desire to be hanged and who committed murder in order to be hanged, could be said to be labouring under a delusion, but not to be insane.

It was all beginning to be a bit confusing and the judge wondered: 'What is the delusion under which you say a man would labour if he committed a murder on purpose to get hanged?'

To which, Mr Harold replied: 'My idea is that he would be a homicidal maniac.'

In his summing up, the judge, Mr Justice Wightman, told the jury that they had to decide whether the prisoner, at the time he committed the act, was or was not a responsible agent.

He said it was not mere eccentricity – not simply because a man acted differently from the rest of mankind – that made him an irresponsible agent. The evidence did show Burton to be a person of irregular habits and a bad apprentice, but the jury was not concerned with irregularity. They had to decide whether or not he knew the nature and quality of the crime he committed in July.

The jury took about a quarter of an hour to reach that decision, returning at about 4.15pm with a guilty verdict.

The judge donned the black cap. The prisoner was asked if he had anything to say and he replied in what a court reporter who was present described as a careless and full tone: 'No sir.'

When the death sentence was pronounced, Burton said: 'Thank you, my lord!' with what that same journalist described as a derisive smile.

He was returned to the prison, where he at once demanded better quality food than he had before, saying he intended to enjoy what time he had left. He was most indignant when he was told he would receive only ordinary gaol diet and thought it specially hard that he was not allowed some tobacco nor permitted to smoke.

On medical advice, however, he was allowed two half pints of porter ale daily.

On Sunday, March 29, he became very unruly and noisy at chapel and declared he would never go there again. That evening he told his gaolers that he was the servant of the Devil and had made up his mind to serve him thoroughly to the end, having nothing more to do with religion and threatening to burn the books he was given to read.

But then, on the following Tuesday, he changed again and accepted the company of the Rev Shirley Woolmer, the gaol chaplain, who he invited to come to pray with him.

He wrote to his sister apologising for his behaviour during a visit she and his aunt made to him in prison and asking her to visit him again, to bring his favourite little nephew, George, and to give his love to their father.

He also wrote to Mrs Houghton, the mother of the boy he murdered, expressing his grief, and she replied saying that she forgave him for what he had done.

His father also wrote to him, conveying his forgiveness, and Burton wrote back, expressing his pleasure at that, and taking the opportunity to pen his father and his brother James a sermon on the fruits of sin and drunkenness.

From that time on he seemed to be very conscious that he had rather a backlog of repentance to catch up on, and he plunged into it with typical passion. He did not expect his life to be spared but he often expressed a wish that he had more time to prepare for death.

He wrote a confession in which he detailed all his wrongs to a number of people. He declared that he had intended to kill the landlady of a public house from which he had been banned but he was afraid he might not succeed, in which case he would have failed in his wish to be hanged. So he determined to find someone else who might be easier to kill first and then to kill the landlady to make quite sure he would be hanged.

On the day of his execution, Burton ate a hearty breakfast. Afterwards, he attended morning service in the gaol, during which he was unable to control his feelings and burst into tears.

At 12.05pm, the chaplains led the way to the scaffold, ahead of the prisoner and the executioner. There were between 5,000 and 6,000 people outside the prison to witness the execution and Burton prayed aloud, first with the chaplains and then alone after they left the platform, leaving him with the executioner.

His last words were: 'Oh Lord, remember me!' Then he dropped to his death.

The newsmen present recorded that the spectators behaved in a most decorous manner 'with no accidents whatever, either to person or pocket, on this melancholy occasion' and scarcely a murmur was heard. When it was over, the crowd dispersed equally quietly.

A BORN LOSER

S TEPHEN Forwood was what we would call today a born loser. Everything he touched turned not to gold, as some of it might have done in other hands, but to trouble, for him and also for others associated with him.

Forwood was born at Ramsgate just after the end of the Napoleonic wars. He claimed his father was a smuggler and his mother a laundress and that they lived at St Lawrence, a village just outside Ramsgate – all of which may have been true.

In any case, his mother died when he was 13 and he apparently then inherited £120 – a useful sum for those days, although he seems not to have had a free hand with it, probably because it was controlled by a guardian. He became a page boy for a while until, in his mid teens, he was apprenticed to a Ramsgate baker.

He was still only 16 when he met a girl called Mary who he later married and whose family set him up with his own baking business in Ramsgate. It should have provided Mary and him with a steady £400 a year income, but it didn't. He and Mary drifted apart. He blamed her 'cold temperament' and he was unfaithful to her after only seven months of marriage.

Slowly but surely, the business slid towards ruin and some 15 months after they were married, it failed completely. With no means of supporting his wife, Forwood left her and went into lodgings in King Street at Ramsgate, with a shop keeper called Ellis, who had been a customer of his.

That could not continue for long though, and soon Forwood left there also and went to London where he hoped to get a clerical job with the South Eastern Railway.

Unhappily however, the job did not materialise and instead he became first a journeyman baker and then a travelling rope

The Ramsgate scene as Stephen Forwood knew it in the 1850s.

salesman, earning a guinea a week.

His parting from Mary seems to have provoked the old maxim that absence makes the heart grow fonder. At any rate, after a while, Mary followed him to London and they lived together again, on and off, for some time. From time to time she returned to Ramsgate and he sometimes visited her there.

But then she became pregnant and their daughter, Emily, was born at St Lawrence. Forwood was with his wife at that time, but he did not stay. Mary and the child rejoined him in London but after more than seven years of this uncertain domesticity (and the birth of another child, a son), little Emily became ill and her mother brought her back to Ramsgate, this time for good.

Mary Forwood went to live with her mother in a house in King Street, opposite where Stephen had lodged for a time, and earned her living as a dressmaker.

Stephen, meanwhile, piled up debts that eventually amounted to £1,800, for which he could have been sent to prison. Desperate to avoid that, he absconded, resolved to start a new life elsewhere.

He went to Bristol, intending to sail for Australia, but instead he moved to Bath, where he began to frequent billiard rooms, which at that time were gambling dens. He knew nothing about the game of billiards, but he found he had a natural talent for it and he began to win bets. By May 1857 he had made enough money to take him to Liverpool where he shared a room with a champion billiards player and made some sort of living playing billiards for money.

He was sending money to his wife and children in Ramsgate whenever he could, which probably was not very often. In Liverpool, he wrote to Mary and told her to advertise any reply in the newspapers, since he was still afraid of being traced and arrested for debt.

After Liverpool, he moved to Dublin and then to Glasgow, slipping further and further towards destitution. In Glasgow he had to sleep rough on the streets and beg for food and was reduced to such a state that he thought seriously of committing suicide.

But then his luck changed. He got a job in a Glasgow billiard room which brought him influential friends and led to his being put in charge of a new yacht club. Another man might have found his feet on that sort of foundation, but not Stephen Forwood. He tried to set himself up in business on his own but he only lost more money and was soon adrift again, this time ending up in Brighton in 1862.

Still owing £1,800, he was now using the name of Ernest Southey to throw his creditors off the scent and he decided the only way of getting himself out of his financial straits was to win the money he needed at the billiard tables.

In February 1863 he thought he had succeeded. With about £150 saved from his winnings, in one night he won no less than £1,700 from the Hon Dudley Ward, younger brother of the Earl of Dudley, in a game of billiards at Kentfield's Billiards Room in Brighton.

It looked like the answer to all his problems and for another man it might have been. But, by whatever name he called himself, he remained the same born loser. In spite of a pre-game agreement that the winner would be paid on the spot, Ward refused to pay. Aggrieved, Southey – as he now called himself – went to friends of Ward, who all assured him he had no need to worry. The Hon Dudley had something of a reputation for not paying his debts and his brother, the earl, always paid them for him to protect the family name. Southey need have no doubts that the earl would pay this debt as well, they said.

But in that too, Southey's luck was out. The earl had decided that enough was enough and that he would bail out his brother no more. He refused point blank to meet the gambling debt.

It was while Southey was beating his breast over this latest of life's injustices that he met Mrs White. He was walking along Brighton seafront one winter's day when he saw a young woman with a desperate expression, going towards the pier.

He recognised the expression as that of a fellow sufferer and guessed that she intended to drown herself. He introduced himself to her, learned that she was a boarding school keeper and mother of four children and that her husband, a teacher, had left her. Her school was running into debt.

Southey could sympathise with her and persuading her not to take her own life after all, he appointed himself her champion, visiting a number of clergymen in the area to try to raise money for her.

He was no more successful on her behalf than he had been on his own, but the two became lovers and he moved in with her and her children.

He continued to demand payment of his debt from both Ward and the earl and to try to recruit sympathetic support from anyone and everyone he hoped would espouse his cause.

It was all to no avail and pursuit of the money owed to him became the consuming obsession of his life. On one occasion, after he resorted to physical violence and was charged with assault, he wrote to one of the national newspapers saying that he would bring his grievance before the entire country in some terrible (but unspecified) way.

Another time, he sent Mrs White to the earl to plead for him, but as soon as the earl discovered what she had come for he had her thrown out. Southey then brought an action against him for assault on Mrs White but although the case achieved some publicity, it only lost more money for Southey.

From August 1864 until June 1865, he and Mrs White lived together in Putney. Southey was by now totally obsessed with getting the money he insisted was owed to him. He wrote long letters to various people, including the Bishop of London, without success and he dogged the earl and his brother wherever he could in an effort to shame one or other of them publicly into paying the debt.

When he and Mrs White were down to their last £40 between them, they resolved on a final desperate bid to collect the money he was owed. They decided they'd live on the £40 until it was all gone and then commit suicide, taking Mrs White's daughter with them, and so excite public opinion that the earl would pay up for the sake of the three surviving children, who would benefit.

Southey broadcast their intention, saying he would sacrifice himself, Mrs White and her four children, his own wife and children and the Earl of Dudley, too – 10 lives in all.

The threat did not have the desired effect and in June 1865 Southey tailed Dudley Ward to Paris and pestered him there, still without success. When he returned to Putney, he found that Mrs White and the children had deserted him. Penniless, he again lived rough for a while, during which time he hatched yet another plan designed to shock the country into recognising his claim and demanding payment on his behalf.

This one he did put into effect.

First, disguised with a beard and moustache, he went to Josiah White at Bedford Terrace, Bow. There he explained that he was inquiring about the whereabouts of Mrs White's three sons, aged nine, 11 and 13, who were now living with their father.

Josiah White was the son of William White the estranged husband of Mrs White and Southey told him that Mrs White wanted the children back.

'Will you get your father to let you bring them to the Opera Hotel in Bow Street?' he asked.

Josiah knew that Southey and Mrs White had been living together and thought they still were. He knew the children were hers, although he didn't know whether or not they were Southey's and he knew all about Southey's claim that he was owed £1,700 by the Hon Dudley Ward. Indeed, anybody who knew Southey and a good many people who did not, now knew about the unpaid debt.

Josiah promised to get in touch with his father about it, whereupon Southey volunteered the information that they planned to take the children with them to Australia.

The next evening, the two men met at the corner of Bedford Row, but Josiah said his father was reluctant to give up the children. However, he promised he would have them the next evening and Southey said he would take the children to Brighton, where Mrs White was staying.

The next evening, Saturday, August 5, 1865, the two men met again in Bedford Row. Josiah suggested they take the children to a public house but Southey could not get accommodation there so he went to Starr's coffee house in Red Lion Street, Holborn, where he hired a room to which the children could be brought.

On Monday, August 7, Josiah brought the children. Southey shook hands with them and took them to the coffee house where he had already booked a room. It was about 10pm and that was the last Josiah saw of them.

Southey took the three boys up to their room and saw them into bed. Next morning, Tuesday, he had breakfast with the children and then asked if they could stay in the coffee room while he had to go out. He was told they could and he went out, staying away all morning, but returning to have dinner and tea with the children.

That evening, he asked for an extra bedroom, saying the eldest boy was poorly. The boy was seen by Eliza Maidman, who worked at Starr's coffee house, and she thought the lad did not look very well. But she thought Southey seemed to be very fond of all three children and he paid for the second room and put the children to bed between 5pm and 6pm, to be out of the way, he explained, because he had some business to attend to.

When he left, he closed the door to room No 8, where the eldest boy was, and locked it. He took the key out of the lock and kept it until he got to the second landing, when he gave it to Eliza as he said goodnight to her. As he came out of No 8, she was about to go into No 6, the other room, when he stopped her, saying: 'It's all right there, Miss.'

On Wednesday morning a chambermaid went to the children's rooms and found all three dead in bed.

The police were called and they found some suspicious bottles which led to investigations that proved the children had each been killed with a spoonful of prussic acid on the Tuesday night.

The Metropolitan Police issued descriptions of Southey which were circulated to police forces throughout the country including the Kent County Constabulary.

Meanwhile Southey had left London and, disguised in his false beard and glasses, travelled to Ramsgate on Wednesday, August 9. He paid 1s 6d for a bed for that night at a house in Bellevue Villas, Ramsgate.

He had not been in touch with his wife, Mary Forwood, for several years by now. Unbeknownst to him, his son had died, but Mary was still at the King Street address and that evening he set out to find her again.

Mary would not let him into her house. He suggested they should go for a walk together, but she wouldn't agree to that, either. Just across the road at No 61, William Ellis was standing at his shop door and Mrs Forwood went across to him. Her husband followed her, still wearing his disguise.

Ellis did not recognise his former lodger until Mrs Forwood told him: 'It's Stephen.' Then, Ellis invited them both in. He and Stephen shook hands and Ellis told Stephen he was glad to see him again.

Stephen told him: 'I have saved up £1,700 but I've been done out of it all.' He told his story once more and then Ellis and his daughter Adelaide, who lived with him, left their visitors alone for a while so they could talk.

It was getting late now though, and after about 15 minutes, the Forwoods left, arranging to meet there again at 8am. Mary went back to her house across the road and Forwood, presumably, returned to his rented room.

As they left, Mary told Ellis that Stephen wanted to see her again at 8am the next day.

'Come and have some breakfast with us,' Ellis invited them both and they thanked him and agreed to do that.

In fact though, Mary arrived early next morning and had her

breakfast before Stephen came, about 20 minutes late for their meeting, saying he had already breakfasted.

Little Emily was playing in the yard when he got there and when she was called in, he asked Mary: 'Is that ours?' Told it was, he embraced the little girl.

Adelaide Ellis suggested that Southey and Mrs Forwood could go upstairs if they had anything to say to each other. Southey wanted to take Emily up with them but she had to be got ready for school first. However, he asked to see her again before she went and about 15 minutes later Adelaide sent the child up.

It was soon after that Adelaide, who was working downstairs, heard two pistol shots, one very quickly after the other. Rushing to the stairs, she saw Emily Forwood rolling down, bleeding profusely. She went to her but Southey reached the child first. He was holding a pistol and he put it to the child's mouth.

Adelaide ran out into the yard, where she screamed to her father, who was working there. As she did so, she heard another, fainter, gunshot from inside the house and that was followed moments later by another, louder, shot.

In the yard, Ellis had heard the shots too, but hadn't taken much notice because some of the local lads were in the habit of firing off guns from time to time. However, when his daughter rushed out, screaming for him to come quickly, he hurried across the yard. As he did so, they both heard another gunshot.

Ellis ran into the house and up the stairs, passing the body of little Emily where it lay on the stairs. He burst in to the room where Southey and his wife were and grabbed Southey by the shoulder. The room was full of smoke and smelled of gunpowder. When the smoke cleared, Ellis saw the body of Mary Forwood lying on the floor.

Ellis' first concern seems to have been for the damage the crime would do to his business of letting rooms and Southey told him he had £1,200 of his own money owed to him which would compensate for what he had done.

Ellis said he would send for the police and Southey replied: 'Yes, that is best. Her troubles are at an end; mine are not. She is better off than ever she was. But as for me, when I return to London I shall be under sentence of death.'

He then took off the glasses and false whiskers he had worn since he arrived back in Ramsgate. The police were called and it was a PC Drayson of Ramsgate Police who arrived and arrested Southey.

As he was led away past the body of the child that was still lying at the bottom of the stairs, Southey's legs gave way and he knelt, taking the dead child's hands in his own. He burst into tears.

At the police station, he asked for pen and paper and he wrote a statement which was later read to magistrates. In it, he said that on August 7 he took three children 'whom I claim as mine by the strongest and holiest ties' to Starr's coffee house.

He went on: 'I felt for these children all the affection a parent could feel. I had utterly worn out and exhausted every power of mind and body in my efforts to secure a home, training and a future for these children, also the other five persons I felt hopelessly dependent upon me. I could struggle and bear up no longer for the last support had been withdrawn from me.

'My sufferings were no longer supportable, my very last hope perished by my bitter and painful experience of our present iniquitously defective social justice and for this I shall be charged with murder.

'I repudiate the charge and charge it back on many who have by their gross and criminal neglect brought about this sad and fearful crisis. I charge back the guilt of these crimes on those high dignitaries of the church and state and justice who have turned a deaf ear to my heart-broken appeals; who have refused to fellow help me in all my frenzied struggles; who have impiously denied the sacred ties of human life, the mutual dependence of man and the fundamental and sacred principles on which our social system itself is based.'

He then went on to name a number of people he blamed for what had happened, including a veritable Who's Who of prominent people: Palmerston, Stanley, Sir Richard Mayne, the Earl of Derby, the Hon Edward Bulwer-Lytton, the Bishop of London, Gladstone, Disraeli and the Earl of Shaftesbury – all because they had failed to reply to his letters about the debt he claimed was owed to him.

He had arrived in Ramsgate wearing spectacles and false whiskers, but now that they were removed several people recognised him as Stephen Forwood, former baker of that town. Nevertheless, he insisted his name was Southey and he refused to answer questions put to Forwood.

He was taken from the magistrates' court to Sandwich gaol to await trial and there, on August 10, he wrote another long statement blaming his crimes on the church and the state for ignoring his pleas for help.

The governor of the gaol at Sandwich, Mr Hill, said that while Southey was in gaol there he had fits or convulsions when he was refused a light at night by visiting magistrates, and on other occasions, too. On those occasions, he seemed to be ill, but he soon recovered.

Southey was tried at Maidstone in December 1865 for the wilful murder of his wife Mary Forwood and Emily his daughter. The Metropolitan Police wanted him to be tried in London for the murder of the White children but the Kent authorities claimed right of possession and he was tried only for the two murders.

The trial began with a wrangle over what the accused should be called. Before the case began an adjournment was requested and granted to allow several witnesses to be present but before the adjournment was actually called, Southey asked if he might be permitted to address the judge for a moment.

The judge explained that either a prisoner or his counsel could address him, but not both, to which Southey replied: 'The point to which I wish to call the attention of the court is with reference to a mistake in the name in which I am arraigned.'

His Lordship ruled that was immaterial, but Southey persisted: 'But there is a vital principle.'

The judge still refused to hear him on the subject and Southey said that placed him in a very difficult position.

'I am not conscientiously able to allow counsel to defend me under the present circumstances,' he protested, but the judge insisted that he had postponed the start of the trial and the prisoner should consider what course he would take. His advice was to allow counsel to continue management of the case.

Southey again tried to speak, but was ordered out of court for the adjournment. When the case was resumed at 1pm that same day, the prisoner was again arraigned under the name of Stephen Forwood. At that, Southey interrupted: 'My Lord, that is not my name. It is Ernest Walter Southey.'

His Lordship repeated that it was immaterial, but agreed that, if he preferred it, the indictment could be ordered to be altered.

And so it was, but when the charge was read with the new name (Southey) and he was asked to plead guilty or not guilty, he said before he could answer he felt bound to place certain information before the court.

We can imagine a certain testiness in the judge's tone as he snapped: 'You must first plead guilty or not guilty.'

Southey said he wished to read a statement, but his Lordship would have none of that.

'You must plead,' he insisted, adding when Southey still hesitated: 'Until you have pleaded I cannot allow you to make any statement.'

After some further exchanges, Southey finally said: 'Then I plead not guilty. May I now be allowed . . . ?'

The judge asked him what was the nature of his application and Southey said he wished to demonstrate that Mrs Forwood's death took place from some other cause than that to which it was now attributed. He declared: 'The verdict upon which I am charged is not a true one. She died before the wounds were inflicted upon her.'

The judge told him that would be decided during the hearing of the case and, after still more exchanges, his Lordship decided he had finally had enough and ordered: 'Will you be good enough now to be silent?'

Southey had still not finished, though. He repeated that he was unable conscientiously to plead unless he was allowed to explain his reasons and when he still refused to plead, the judge ordered a plea of not guilty to be recorded and the case proceeded with.

With one last attempt at delay, Southey now applied for a special jury, to which his Lordship replied quite shortly: 'You cannot have one!'

One of the witnesses was William Ellis who said Southey had always seemed to him to be a quiet, inoffensive man and although he was separated from his wife, she continued to be very fond of him: a statement which provoked an outburst of ramblings from the prisoner, during which he was held down by two turnkeys. However, after drinking a glass of water, he recovered himself and the case continued.

When Southey's lawyer was about to cross-examine Ellis, Southey interrupted, saying he could not conscientiously allow anyone to appear for him.

He told the court: 'I seek to lay the whole truth before the court, but I cannot do it as I have not the facility for doing so.'

Another exchange took place between prisoner and judge, at the end of which the judge said he would ask the jury to decide whether or not Southey was in a fit state to take his trial. Shortly after that, the proceedings were adjourned until the next day and the jury was locked up for the night.

Southey's defence lawyer tried to persuade the jury that Southey was not of sound mind when he committed the murders. He called medical witnesses to support that and one, Dr James Dulvey, physician of New Brompton, said a long conversation he had with Southey left him under the impression that his mind was thoroughly unhinged.

Mr F. Fry, senior surgeon to the West Kent Hospital at Maidstone, said he judged Southey to be of unsound mind in which he did not believe murder to be a crime. On the other hand, Major Bannister, governor of Maidstone gaol, said Southey appeared to him to be a very intelligent man, perfectly coherent and rational. However, he did agree the prisoner had protested against being taken to the prison chapel, saying he was of no faith and certainly did not belong to the Church of England.

At the end of the case, after the judge's summing up, the jury retired for about ten minutes, returning to say they found the accused to be of sound and sane mind, and guilty as charged. Southey heard the verdict quite calmly, despite an outburst of applause in court which was quickly checked.

As the judge was about to don the black cap, Southey said, quite calmly: 'I wish to ask a question, my lord. I wish to know what are my privileges.'

The judge told him he might say anything in arrest of judgement but not question the verdict, whereupon the prisoner embarked upon a speech in which he said he understood he might address the court and asked for two slates on which he had made some notes to be returned to him.

Asked if he wished to raise any points of law, he became silent and the judge then passed the death sentence.

Further efforts were made on Southey's behalf to obtain a stay of execution in order to enquire further into the state of his mind and Southey himself wrote to the Home Secretary and to Mr Justice Mellor, the judge in the case, complaining of the illegality of his trial because he had been refused permission to plead his own case.

He continued to insist that he was not insane however and asked for his case to be argued before metaphysicians and philosophers.

He complained about not being left alone in his cell, where he said he wished to be alone with God. He wrote tirelessly about his life, charging society with his crimes, and he cherished copies of some 200 letters written to various people although he denied having written a threatening letter to Charles Dickens.

As the date set for his execution drew near, his demeanour changed and he expressed forgiveness of the Earl of Dudley and others and withdrew his charge against society. On his last Sunday he confessed fully to his crimes, accepting the moral as well as the actual blame.

He wrote: 'I desire to acknowledge openly that the overwhelming mass of troubles to which I have been subjected and which have been the means of bringing me to a sad and untimely end, are closely traceable to my having lost in my earlier years the guiding and soothing belief of the truths of the Christian religion. I desire to acknowledge before all men my heartfelt and deeply sorrowful sense of my utter sinfulness.'

In spite of that, he still said he had done the right thing in committing the murders and when asked if he acknowledged the justice of the sentence he said emphatically: 'No!'

He asked to be allowed to see the warrant for his execution, which he read carefully before handing it back. At the scaffold, he shook hands with the prison governor and the chaplain.

The crowd of spectators in front of the prison was not large, partly because the execution was conducted during a heavy fall of snow, but also because new rules had made executions less of a spectacle now and crowds were, in any case, smaller than they had been in the past.

The Maidstone Journal described the effect of the new procedures: 'The scaffold was hung round with black cloth to such a height that when the drop fell only just the top of the convict's head was visible to the crowd. The body, after hanging for an hour, was cut down and a cast of the head taken. In the afternoon the body was buried within the precincts of the gaol.'

Stephen Forwood – or Ernest Walter Southey, as he insisted on being called – gave the impression, during his trial, that he would have appreciated a bigger audience at the end. But, if that were the case, he was denied that as well, remaining a born loser to the end.

A Woman Scorned

I F it is ever possible to say just when the seeds of tragedy are
first sown in any life, then it might be said they were sown in
the life of Ann Lawrence when she was taken into the home
of Walter Highams and his wife at Maidstone.

Ann was a pretty teenager when her mother died and her father
could not look after her. She left his home at Farningham in Kent
and came to the Highamses as a house servant. Her employer was
very much older than she was; a greengrocer in Stone Street, he
had been married for 15 years.

In the light of what happened later, it may be that Highams
took a rather too lively interest in the young servant girl and she
may not have been an altogether unwilling recipient of his atten-
tions. At any rate, she left the house after only five or six weeks
and was married a year later to Stephen Lawrence and went to
live with him in Gravesend.

And that, it might have seemed, was that. But some five or six
years later, Highams' wife left him. He was now in business as a
market gardener and general dealer, a business that took him to
various towns, including Gravesend and Town Malling (now
called West Malling) and it was in the latter that he had a lady
friend, a Miss Eaglington, who he had known for several years
and who may well have been the reason why his wife left him.

In the course of his travels, he and Ann Lawrence met again.
She now had a son, Jeremiah, known as Jesse, but it wasn't long
after she met Highams again that she left her husband and took
the child to live in Greenwich, where Highams visited her about
once a fortnight and, in fact, supported her while she lived there
and he worked in Malling.

It was a happy enough liaison and after about 18 months they went to live together at No 2 Ebury Cottages, Tunbridge Wells. By this time Ann's son was nearly four years old and she and Highams had a child of their own, a six month old baby. They were, in the main, a very happy couple.

But then, round about Christmas 1865, Ann learned for the first time that she was not the only woman in Highams' life. It was about 10 one night when Miss Eaglington arrived at No 2 Ebury Cottages to see 'her' Walter and Ann learned about her lover's relationship with the other woman – a relationship that had borne them two children already and Miss Eaglington was again pregnant by Highams.

Ann was furious. She hit out at the other woman, blacking her eye, and then picked up a knife, threatening to do even more serious damage. Highams had to intervene and hold the two women apart while he did what he could to calm them both.

Eventually, the other woman was persuaded to leave the house and only then did Ann calm down. But she changed towards her lover from that time. She had always been very fond of him but now she became jealous and suspicious and nagged him continually about where he had been and what he had been doing.

Things came to head on Wednesday April 11, 1866, when Ann agreed to travel to London for Highams to buy a ton of carrots for his business. She was supposed to be staying the night in London and travelling home the next morning, so she left the baby with a neighbour. Highams and a friend of his were at the station to see her off on the train to London.

As soon as Ann was safely on her way though, he and his partner, another man called Hall, left Tunbridge Wells to deliver two bags of feathers to a customer in Malling and thinking that Ann would not be home that night, Highams did not bother to return home either. Instead he stayed the night in Malling.

When Ann came home that evening between 8 and 9pm and found that Highams was away, she at once assumed the worst and was very angry indeed. She went to her neighbour, Maria Taylor, and asked if she had seen anything of him. Maria said she had not and Ann stormed out and walked along the street to see if she could find out from anyone else where he was. When she returned, she told Maria he had gone to Malling to see the other woman.

A police constable of the period. This constable served at Goudhurst, Kent in 1870–80 (Picture: Kent Police Museum).

'I'll have his life, sure as he's a man!' she stormed.

Maria made her a cup of tea and advised Ann to go home to bed and wait for Walter to come home. Ann drank the tea and by the time she went to her own home, she was still very angry but calmer.

Highams came back to Tunbridge Wells next day, during the afternoon, and found Ann waiting for him near a beer shop in the London Road. As he said afterwards 'She was very cross with me! She blowed me up for staying out all night.'

They went home together and had tea, during which Ann was very quiet. She remained quiet all the rest of the evening. Highams had taken little Jeremiah out with him all day on his barrow and he had fallen down in the mud and dirtied his clothes, for which his mother beat him.

On Friday night, Ann and Walter again quarrelled. Their words could be heard clearly by the neighbours who heard Ann telling him she would 'pay him' for going to Malling.

That night, Ann went to bed first after sending the boy to his room in the front of the house. Highams followed her at about 10pm. All four of them slept in that one room because the other bedroom was being used to store apples. Jeremiah slept at the bottom of the bed and the baby shared it with its parents.

It was between 4 and 5am on Saturday when Ann got up. Highams later said he couldn't be sure what time it was because there was no clock in the house. But it was just beginning to get light and Ann told him: 'I have been in such trouble all night; I will go down and make myself a cup of tea.'

She went down only partly dressed and Highams, who usually got up at about 6.30, after Ann had got his breakfast for him, went back to sleep with the baby on his arm. When he woke up again it was to find Ann chopping at him with a billhook in both hands. In trying to defend himself, and the baby, two of his fingers were chopped off.

Ann told him: 'I have killed one, I will kill you, all three!'

Highams shouted: 'Murder!' and told her to leave off, but she would not. He managed to get up from the bed and he grappled with her but the force of the blows he had already received had weakened him and she was still striking him.

At last, though, she stopped and went downstairs. When he followed, sliding down the stairs because he was too weak to walk, she turned and renewed the attack with the billhook.

Then she threw the weapon aside and seized him by the hair and began to knock his head against the wall, shouting and screaming that she would kill him.

The noise of the rumpus next door was heard by Maria Taylor. She heard Highams' screams of: 'Murder!' and she looked at her watch. It was 5.40am. She got up and went downstairs to find Ann Lawrence in the yard. Ann then had on an apron and a black-stuff dress. She was calling to Higham: 'You dirty . . . ! See what you have brought yourself to. I told you I would do it, for live like this I won't.'

When she saw Maria, she told her: 'He has killed my child. It is not his and he never liked it.'

Earlier at about 5.30, John Allen, a labourer who lived in Martin's Row, the back yard of which overlooked the front of Ebury Cottages, also heard the screams of: 'Murder!' and went outside to see what was happening. He saw Ann come out of her house, her chest and arms covered in blood, and go to a pump in the yard to wash herself. She saw him and told him: 'Go for the police, I will give myself up.'

Without yet knowing quite why the police needed to be called, but fearful of the story he guessed the blood might tell, Allen was on his way to fetch a policeman when he met Edmund Cary, a bricklayer of Union Place and Edward Vigor, a painter, who also lived nearby. They too had heard the commotion in No 2 Ebury Cottages as they passed and they had looked in through the front room window and seen Ann pummelling Highams' head against the wall. When she saw them, she rushed out of the door, which was when she was seen by Allen.

The other two men saw that there was blood all over the room and on the front of the woman. When Ann came into the yard she was only partly coherent but they understood her to say that Highams had cut the throat of her child, who was dead, and she had tried to kill him. She left them in no doubt that she was only sorry she had not succeeded.

When her victim staggered out of the house behind her, he was still in his nightshirt. He too begged them to go for the police for, he said, there was murder in the house. Ann, turning on him, called him a villain and a rogue and said he had murdered her child.

The policeman who arrived at the scene, PC May, went into the Highams' house and upstairs to the front bedroom where he saw a child lying on its back. Its head was on the pillow, near the door at the foot of the bed, its throat cut and the blade of a razor still embedded in the wound. The body was still warm, but the neck was nearly cut right through.

When Ann saw him bring the child down the stairs, she cried: 'My child, my child. I want my child.'

The PC said the child's throat was cut and it was dead, but Ann replied: 'Not my child. My child is alive and lying on the pillow.'

The constable went back upstairs and brought down the baby and gave it to Ann, who asked Maria to take it for her. She said the dead child was hers but not his, adding: 'He has killed it and meant to kill me but I was too quick for him.'

She admitted wounding Highams and said she was sorry she hadn't done for him.

A doctor was called and Highams' wounds were washed before he was taken to the infirmary where he remained for the next 14 weeks. Two of his fingers had to be amputated.

He had 13 wounds altogether: four on the head, four on the shoulder, four on the right hand and one on the left arm. Despite his injuries though, he was never very close to death.

Ann Lawrence was arrested by Police Superintendent Embery at about 6.30 that morning. She remained quite calm when charged with the murder of her son, Jeremiah, saying: 'I want to go. What the man Higham got, I gave him. I intended to kill him and I'm very sorry I didn't. But I didn't kill the child.'

As she was speaking, a friend of Highams, a man called Hollands, arrived at the house. Seeing him, Ann lost her calm and became very excited.

'Don't let that man come in here,' she shouted. 'He shan't come in. He has been the cause of all this. He has been with Walter several times to Malling to another woman he has.'

She was taken to the police station where she said: 'Highams took me away from my husband two years ago and I have recently found out there is a woman at Malling who has had several children by him.'

Later on the same day, a coroner's inquest was held at Highams' hospital bedside, where Ann was taken under guard. She stood smiling through the whole hearing and when asked what she was smiling at she said it was a pleasure to her to see Highams so badly injured, although she would rather have killed him.

The coroner concluded that little Jeremiah had been wilfully murdered by his mother and she was committed for trial at the assizes in Maidstone.

There, she continued to deny that she had killed her son. If that were true, of course, the only conclusion to be drawn was that Highams had killed the boy. However, as the judge reminded the jury, there could be no doubt that one of the two had killed the child, but they did not have to decide whether or not Highams was guilty of the crime, but only whether or not Ann Lawrence was.

The evidence was against her. Richard Davey, the house surgeon at Tunbridge Wells Infirmary, said he did not believe the blood on Lawrence's apron came from Highams. In his opinion, the blood came from a large vessel – it looked as though blood had been poured on it from a watering can.

But no vessel of any size had been severed in Highams' body. Although he had lost a lot of blood and his shirt was saturated with it, the surgeon believed that Highams' blood had left different stains on Lawrence's clothes.

If the man had killed the child, he said, there must have been blood on his shirt, but he couldn't say if any of the blood on the shirt was in fact the child's.

The defence lawyer used the case to illustrate what he called 'the serious evils which characterise the administration of the criminal law in this country'. Lawrence was on trial and could not speak for herself, whereas Highams had been able to give his version of events and in doing so inevitably piled the blame on to Lawrence.

Yet Lawrence had all along insisted that she did not kill the boy. The medical evidence was inconclusive.

At the end of the trail, it took the jury about three hours to decide that she was indeed guilty. Asked if she had anything to say, Lawrence said she had not had an opportunity to make any statement before the magistrates nor the coroner.

She went on to say: 'I never killed my child. I shall die with a clear conscience. I never killed him; that I can swear with a clear conscience before God or man. There is no proper grounds to convict me of the charge.'

Nevertheless, sentence of death was passed. The judge said it appeared the prisoner had imbibed a feeling of jealousy against Walter Highams – of whose conduct he would not say one word (!) but he thought that, having taken her from her home he might have conducted himself towards her with more kindness and consideration than he had done.

When the judge ended with the words: '. . . and may the Lord have mercy upon your soul,' Lawrence responded: 'I hope He will, my Lord. I did not do it.'

She said she wished she could have had the privilege of cross-examining Highams in the court because, if she had, she would not have been found guilty. She insisted she was not guilty.

Ann Lawrence was still not yet 30 years old and an attempt was made to get her sentence commuted. A petition was sent to the Home Office, but after her insistence up to the time of her sentencing that she had not killed the boy, on the Sunday following her conviction, just before Christmas 1866, she asked to see the prison governor to whom she confessed her guilt.

She was executed at Maidstone one Thursday morning early in January 1867. It was an event that aroused unusual interest, even at a time when executions were regarded as major public spectacles.

For one thing, it was the first execution that Maidstone had witnessed for almost a year, since Southey was hanged there in 1865 (see chapter nine).

For another thing, it was the first execution of a woman since the new gallows were built at Maidstone more than 30 years before, in 1834.

Exceptional curiosity was always provoked by the murder of a young child, especially when the death was caused by the child's own mother.

And, finally, for good measure, this was a double execution which Ann Lawrence shared with another convicted murderer, James Fletcher (see chapter eleven).

For all these reasons, it was not altogether surprising that there was a crowd of several thousand people gathered outside the gates of Maidstone prison that January morning to witness the last moments of the life and the death of Ann Lawrence.

JAILHOUSE MURDER

THE man who shared the gallows with Ann Lawrence at Maidstone on January 10, 1867, was James Fletcher, a former Derbyshire miner, 20 years old, six ft tall and an ex-Guardsman.

He had enlisted in the Foot Guards in 1864 and had soon gained something of a reputation as a hard-drinking womaniser. It was predictable that he would get into trouble of some sort and it happened when, with a group of other soldiers, he was drinking in a public house in the company of a known prostitute who was robbed of a gold watch she had.

Although there were others involved, Fletcher was left 'holding the can'. He was convicted for the offence and sentenced to seven years penal servitude, but he believed he had been unjustly singled out for punishment while his companions escaped scot-free and he harboured a grudge against the system generally all the time he was in prison.

One of his chief complaints was about prison food, which he always regarded as inadequate. More than once he was disciplined for consuming his allowance of gruel and then hiding his bowl and pretending he had not had any.

After serving part of his sentence, he was sent to St Mary's Isle at Chatham, where he was set to work as a dockyard labourer and it was while he was there, on September 1, 1866, that he quarrelled with another convict about a shovel.

The party he was with was under the supervision of a 'trusty' called James Boyle, who reported Fletcher to one of the prison officers. As a result, Fletcher was ordered to be confined on a bread and water diet for two days. To a big man with Fletcher's appetite, it was a severe punishment indeed.

Maidstone prison today.

When he was released again, he joined a gang of about 20 other convicts at work in the dockyard, again under the supervision of the 'trusty', Boyle, with another man, Irvine, on guard over them with a musket and bayonet.

The men had worked all day at the monotonous and tiring work of stonebreaking and at about 5pm Fletcher saw an opportunity to have his revenge on Boyle for reporting him on the previous occasion.

With his stonebreaking hammer, he attacked the 'trusty', dealing him a heavy blow on the temple that felled him to the ground. To emphasise his disaffection, Fletcher added two more blows, one of which smashed Boyle's nose and the other the side of his face.

The guard, Irvine, rushed at Fletcher and attacked him with his bayonet, at which Fletcher immediately dropped his hammer and surrendered.

Boyle was rushed to hospital, where he lived for a day or two without regaining consciousness before he died.

Fletcher was unrepentant. He made no attempt to deny his guilt, saying he was tired of the life he was living, being starved to death and confined to his cell when Boyle informed on him. He took the opportunity to complain that all the convicts were starving and were drinking oil or anything else they could steal just to keep themselves alive.

His trial at Maidstone was very much an open and shut affair. There was no doubt he was responsible for Boyle's death and he was found guilty of murder by a jury that scarcely needed to confer before returning its verdict.

Fletcher was resigned to his fate from the start, but he did express his regrets and sympathy for the family of the man he had killed who was perhaps as much a victim of the harshness of prison life in the 1860s as of his killer's vengefulness and uncertain temper.

THE DOVER PRIORY MURDER

THE fairly brief life of 18 year old Dover railway carriage cleaner Thomas Wells was not particularly notable. He was a rather quiet lad, of good family and regular in his churchgoing. When he started work at Dover Priory railway station he was, at first, a helpful and willing worker but after a while that changed.

His father blamed the character change on an accident to his son who, in the summer of 1867, suffered head and chest injuries and was taken home semi-conscious after he became trapped between the buffers of a carriage and an engine.

Others who also noticed the change blamed it on the fact that young Wells had to work on Sundays, so that he stopped going to church altogether and fell into bad ways.

His employers denied any knowledge of an accident that would have accounted for the young man's changed behaviour. Whatever the reason, Wells became aggressive and eccentric in his behaviour and considerably less reliable than he had been.

The station master at Dover Priory station was Edward Adolphus Walshe; a kindly enough man but a stern disciplinarian who began to find frequent cause to warn or threaten Wells, until the youngster became convinced he was being deliberately victimised.

In April he was particularly resentful when he was told to collect a cartful of manure and take it to the station master's garden. He refused to do it at first, saying that such work was no part of his duties. Walshe reported him to his superior, Henry Cox, Superintendent at the station, although Cox took no action, probably

Members of the Dover Borough police force in the second half of the 19th century. (Courtesy of the Kent Police Museum.)

privately judging that Wells had a point when he said it was not his job to cart manure for the station master's private garden.

It was soon after that however, that Wells took a pistol with him to work. It was one he had bought from one of the carriage examiners, John Mitchell, some nine months earlier. He had also bought some gunpowder and percussion caps in the town and he and Mitchell had taken it in turns to fire the gun behind one of the engine sheds. When all the gunpowder and caps were used up, Wells put the gun back into its box and locked it.

The station master, Walshe, was furious when he heard about the gunplay at his station and he warned Wells never to do such a thing again. It was a reprimand that was to have fatal consequences.

Wells took his tongue-lashing and then, when Walshe had stalked off back to his office, the youngster turned to others in the porters' room and commented: 'I'll let that old bugger have the contents of it!'

An engine driver, John Prescott, who was among those present, told Wells not to be such a fool.

'If anyone else heard you say that,' he said, 'you'd be locked up for threatening behaviour.'

Wells, however, only repeated his threat, although a little while later when Walshe returned to the porters' room and asked what he had done with the gun, Wells said he had thrown it away.

Walshe was not satisfied with that though. He told Wells: 'You will have to go down to see Mr Cox this time.'

The exchange was interrupted by the arrival of the evening express from London. Wells had to board the train every evening to travel with it the extra mile to Dover Harbour station, where he cleaned out the carriages ready for their return to Victoria.

He and Walshe both headed for the train. Wells went into the brake van while Walshe got into an empty first class compartment but then changed his mind and pushed the door shut, remaining on the platform as the train pulled out again.

Leaving Dover Priory station, the train went almost immediately into a tunnel and just before the brake van followed it into the darkness, Wells jumped out, landing just short of the platform, and walked back to the station. He was seen by the station master, Walshe, who was outraged at this blatant display of disobedience.

He stormed along the platform to confront Wells and asked him why he had left the train. Wells replied that he was not going down there (to the Harbour station) to be made a bloody fool of.

Walshe had finally had enough. 'It's gone too far!' he exploded. 'I'll telegraph headquarters.'

At 6.30 the following morning, May 1, 1868, Wells was at work as usual in the carriage shed. The London express was due to leave within two hours. A fellow employee, 12 year old Charles Sinclair of the loco department, commented: 'I thought you had to go down to the Harbour.'

Wells told him: 'I got in the brake van but as soon as we got to the tunnel, I jumped out and if that old bugger (Walshe) says much more to me today, I'll shoot him.'

He had brought with him from home an old fowling gun his father had given him to scare birds from his garden and during the morning he absented himself from work to buy four penny worth of gunpowder from an ironsmith's shop in Snargate Street.

Later that morning, Wells was called to the station office to be confronted by the Superintendent, Henry Cox. Station master Walshe was also present, demanding at the very least a full apology from Wells.

Wells was given ten minutes to decide whether or not he would apologise. The alternative, he was told, was to be fined or fired.

The young man left the office to make up his mind what it would be. One of the porters, John Golding, asked him what had happened and Wells told him, adding that if he had to leave, 'the old bugger' would know about it.

When, at the end of his ten minutes, he went back to the station master's office, Wells did not apologise. He remained surly and aggressive and when he left again Cox and Walshe had to decide what punishment would be appropriate.

While they were discussing it, Wells reappeared. He pushed the office door open, stepped inside and raised the fowling piece he held in his hand, ready to fire. He walked towards the station master and, at almost point-blank range, blew out the station master's brains.

He made no real effort to escape. He only ran across the station and hid himself in a second class railway compartment. But he was seen to climb into the compartment by several of the men working at the station. Cox called the police, while another man was sent for a doctor.

Police Sergeant George Stevens arrived at the station and went to the carriage where Wells was known to be hiding. He opened the door and found Wells crouching inside, his right arm on the seat and the gun in his left hand.

He made no attempt to resist arrest. Asked to hand over the gun, he did so and when, in response to the sergeant's request to him to get out of the carriage, he put his head out of the door, Sgt Stevens took his arm and, together with Mr Cox, helped the lad down.

He was taken to the police station where, charged with causing the death of Mr Walshe, he made no reply.

He was duly brought to trial at Maidstone Summer Assizes where his defence barrister claimed the injuries received in the accident had influenced his mind.

The jury, however, took only five minutes to decide upon a

verdict of wilful murder and Mr Justice Willis donned the black cap.

He told Wells: 'You have been convicted on the clearest evidence of a terrible murder, committed under the circumstances of atrocity so great as to be almost incredible. You have been rightly convicted; no-one can entertain the slightest doubt. I would warn you to give up all hopes of this world and turn with bitter repentance to a God of mercy in whose sight the best of us are nothing and whom the worse need not despair.'

Wells had become a public figure through the police sheets of the day, which wallowed in the sensational details of the case.

Until this time, ever since public executions had been moved from Penenden Heath, prisoners had been executed, first on temporary gallows erected over the prison entrance and then on the gallows that were set up next to the porter's lodge outside the main entrance to Maidstone prison.

During the 38 years after the end of executions on Penenden Heath up to 1868, Maidstone had witnessed 28 executions there, including those of two women.

Under a new Act of 1868, however, the new gallows had to be built inside the prison walls and sited where it could not be seen, neither from the prison cells nor from nearby houses overlooking the prison. A former timber yard was chosen as the site. It had a high wall of its own and an iron roof was built over one part of the yard, with the gallows beneath it. The necessary pit was dug under the trap to take the falling body.

Wells spent the last weeks of his life writing more than a hundred letters, reading and attending to the ministrations of Sugden Frazer, the prison chaplain. He wrote to Henry Cox and to the widow of Edward Walshe, asking for their forgiveness for the great wrong he had done and he also wrote several letters to the girl he had hoped to marry, in which he said he hoped they might meet again in heaven.

The execution took place on Thursday, August 13, 1868, with William Calcraft officiating as executioner and George Smith his assistant. Calcraft had been in his job for almost 40 years, but was not very good at it. He was infamous for a series of bungled hangings, many because he favoured a short drop which some-

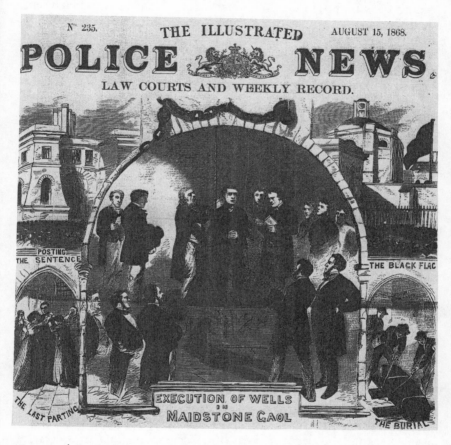

The execution of Thomas Wells as depicted by *The Illustrated Police News* in August 1868.

times resulted in the condemned man slowly choking to death.

The new Act gave the High Sheriff, who was obliged to be present, the discretion of allowing members of the press to witness the execution and, in fact, 16 journalists were present when Wells died. Because it was the first execution to be carried out other than in full view of the general public, there was a large contingent of the London press men present.

A rumour had circulated in the town that 200 people would be admitted by ticket, but it was quite untrue. Executioner Calcraft was described as wearing the same greasy suit and buttonhole flower he had worn to earlier executions. Smith, a tall, thin, wiry man with a keen eye, his cheeks and part of his forehead shaved, wore a velveteen shooting coat, loose trousers and a billycock hat. One observer described him as looking like an acrobat who had donned his private clothes over his professional costume.

Journalists reported that the culprit prayed fervently with the Rev Mr Frazer, the chaplain, for a few moments and as the drop fell he was singing in a loud voice the 486th hymn. He appeared to die after two or three convulsive struggles.

Outside the prison, some 40 or 50 people 'of the lowest class' assembled but there was little excitement among them. As the drop fell, a black flag was hoisted over the entrance gate near to where the old drop had been and a notice was fixed outside the prison walls, as required by the new law.

The notice read: 'We, the undersigned, hereby declare that judgement of death was this day executed upon Thomas Wells, in our presence.'

The notice was signed by R. Furley, Under Sheriff; C.W. Bannister, Governor; W.F.C.S Frazer, Chaplain.

The legally required inquest was held at about 3pm that same day before County Coroner J.N. Dudlow and a jury. It returned a verdict that the deceased was hanged in pursuance of a conviction for murder.

THE BODY
IN THE BARN

O N January 8, 1867, Mary Ann Bridger left her parents' home in Luton Road, Margate, where she sometimes lived – sometimes, because she was in the habit of staying away from home all night and on those occasions it seems likely she spent the time with a much older man called Thomas Fordred.

On that particular day, however, she had been at home all day, until 5pm when she went out. She was tidily if poorly dressed when she left, wearing a skirt and blouse with a shawl over her shoulders. She went to the Liverpool Arms in Margate where, in fact, she met her parents again when they went in there later on.

By then she was with Fordred. He was a 48 year old labourer whose wife had died. Mary, who was 27, and he had known each other for about three years and he had visited the family home once but her mother did not like him and he never repeated the visit.

Mrs Bridger bought her daughter a glass of beer in the Liverpool Arms and Mary returned the gesture by buying her mother some rum. They were all fairly sober at this point, although Mary and Fordred had been drinking rum together before her parents arrived.

Fordred was a rough sort of fellow. He had certainly hit Mary at least once and that in sight of her mother, which was one of the reasons why she did not like him. On this particular night he was overheard by another customer to tell Mary: 'If I catch you going with any other man I'll knock your brains out.'

But he was also heard to speak in a more friendly way to her, calling her his 'old daisy' and suggesting they went home together for 'a good feed'.

Her parents left the pub before Mary and Fordred did but they saw each other again later on, this time in Victoria Road. It was the last time her mother saw Mary alive.

Evidently, Fordred took Mary shopping for food because they were seen by a patrolling policeman to go into a shop in Victoria Road and come out again with some packages, which they put down on the pavement. Some potatoes rolled out of one of the packages and Fordred swore at Mary because of that. The policeman told them to move on and they did so, going in the direction of Salmstone Farm on the south west outskirts of the town.

It was a clear, moonlit night, although very cold, so the constable could see them both clearly as they walked away and he had no doubt that both had been drinking. Fordred at least could not walk straight. But they seemed to be on good terms and apart from the coarseness with which Fordred spoke to Mary when the potatoes spilled out of the bag, they were not quarrelling.

The road Mary and Fordred took would have led them under a railway bridge before they reached the farm, but quite what happened along the way can only be conjectured. However, at some time between 10 and 11 that night, Ann Emptage heard an angry voice threatening: 'I'll do for you!' and then heard someone come into her cottage at Salmstone Farm.

Her husband George was wagonner at Salmstone Grange and he was out of the house at the time, but Mrs Emptage heard her cottage door open and when, a few minutes later, she went to see who it was, she saw there were some unfamiliar clothes in her washhouse. The washhouse door was, in fact, also the front door to the cottage.

She did not see who had come in and left the clothes there but she did recognise the shawl because she had seen Mary Bridger wearing it a few days before. Now there was fresh snow and blood on it.

A few minutes later, Mrs Emptage saw Fordred, who she knew, going towards the stable.

In the stable, Fordred found George Emptage. They knew each other and Fordred said: 'Hey, come and help me get old Poll up, will you? She's lying on the bank, drunk.'

George noticed that Fordred had blood on his face and on the front of his jacket so he stopped what he was doing and went back to the road, between the railway bridge and the farm. It was only two or three minutes' walk and there, sure enough, lay Mary Bridger, almost nude with just a few rags left on her.

The road had recently been mended and there were a lot of loose flint stones lying about which George thought might have explained the blood on Fordred's face and clothes.

George helped lift Mary on to Fordred's shoulder and they walked back to the barn together. There, George decided he'd done his bit and left the two together. He judged Fordred to be 'about half drunk'.

Some time later, Fordred came to the stable again and told George Emptage he was going for the police.

As he walked back towards the town, Fordred met another man he knew, a labourer like himself, called Thomas Fuller. As the men met, Fordred told Fuller: 'Old Poll's done it this time.'

Fuller didn't understand. 'Done what?' he asked.

'Killed herself!'

Fuller noticed that Fordred had blood on his left ear and he asked: 'Have you got blood on your hands?'

Fordred said he had not. 'I got the wagonner to help me get her on to my shoulder and I took her to the barn,' he said. 'But then I found she was cold and dead. I gave her a kiss and left her.'

With that, Fordred went on into town. When he reached Margate police station he found a police constable on duty outside.

'Is there anyone inside?' he asked.

'No,' replied the constable.

'Then can I speak to you?' Fordred asked. Told he could, he went on: 'You know my old Poll? I met her and we had two half pints of beer and two half-quarters of rum and then went to the Liverpool Arms where we had four half-quarters of rum. Then we went to Mr Payne's shop and afterwards left for Salmstone.

'I was half drunk and she was three-parts drunk. She fell down near the railway arch and I picked her up. Then she fell down again and I fell on top of her.

'I didn't like to see her lying there – she would have frozen to

A group of members of the Kent County Constabulary in the 1880s. (Courtesy of the Kent Police Museum.)

death. So I picked her up and went and called the wagonner to help me. I took her to the barn and got some straw and covered her up. I thought she was dead. Her face was cold and I couldn't hear her breathing. I'm quite certain she's dead now and I've come straight down to you.

'It was no good for me to run away with all this blood on my clothes because I know I would soon be brought back again.'

The constable asked how he got the blood on his clothes and Fordred told him: 'By carrying her.'

They went into the police station then, where Fordred was detained until the Station Superintendent could be brought.

To him, Fordred said Mary's clothes had come off as he helped her up and he was very sorry she should have come to such an end. As he himself put it:

'She was a bad 'un, I know, but she's been a good old gal to me.'

The wagonner's wife, Mrs Emptage, afterwards said that the clothes she found in her washhouse were very old and thin and tore very easily when she picked them up, so it is not entirely impossible that Fordred's drunken fumblings as he tried to pick Mary up could have ripped the clothes off her unintentionally.

But when the body was examined early next morning, the doctor found two large wounds at the back of her head and some marks of violence on her chest and collar bone.

Later that day, police investigations at the place where Mary apparently died revealed evidence that suggested there had been quite a struggle in which some of the contents of the packages they had been carrying had spilled out and there was what might have been a handful of hair lying in the road, apparently pulled from the head of Mary Bridger.

It was enough to bring Fordred before magistrates, who decided it was enough, too, to justify sending him for trial at the Maidstone Spring Assizes in March, where he was charged with the wilful murder of Mary Bridger.

Medical evidence was given by a Margate surgeon who had inspected the body in the barn, where it had been covered with straw and a few bits of clothing. He said he found several wounds: the upper lip was cut and a tooth had been loosened; there were bruises on the collar bone and two deep wounds in the scalp that appeared to have been caused with a blunt instrument. There were bruises, too, on the backs of the hands, as if they had been trodden on and marks on the skin suggested she had been kicked by a boot with rows of hobnails in it. There were also other bruises on the front and back of the body and internal ruptures as well.

The injuries could not, the surgeon declared, have been caused by a fall. Fordred claimed they were caused when Mary repeatedly fell down as he tried to help her up, but the prosecution ridiculed that idea, saying it was too unreasonable to be entertained by a jury.

In his summing up, the judge said the really disputable matters appeared to him to be singularly few. It was certain that on the night of January 8, Mary Ann Bridger came to her end. It was certain, also, that her death was caused by injuries she had received and that the prisoner was in her company up to the time of her death.

The question was: 'Did he inflict those injuries?'

The judge remarked on an angry voice that was heard to threaten: 'I'll do for you' and said that, without any disrespect to Margate, he thought it might be quite possible that more than one drunk and angry person might be making his way late at night along a road so near the town.

He thought the overheard threat earlier during the evening that if Mary went out with any other man, Fordred would knock her brains out might be taken as a rough way of stating affection for her. But the unfeeling language in which he told Fuller about the poor woman's death formed a picture of apparent hard-heartedness.

At the same time, though, a man might appear unfeeling in speaking of the death of a woman he had loved without having been instrumental in causing her death.

The judge told the jury he honestly thought the prisoner's own statement made a manslaughter verdict practically impossible. The verdict, in his judgement, must be guilty of murder or else not guilty.

In fact, it was guilty. The jury was out for 15 minutes before returning with its verdict and as he donned the black cap the judge told Fordred: 'You took the life of one to whom you were bound by the ties of closest relationship. You took it cruelly, savagely, without pity and without remorse. The law is more merciful to you than you were to her.'

In a statement made in prison, Fordred said: 'The woman must have met her death by my means, but I never had the slightest intention of killing her. I was rough with her and made her stand on her feet and we fell backwards together several times. There must have been a good deal of rough treatment, but there were no blows and I solemnly declare that I never once kicked her.'

He persisted in that version of events to the end and there were many who believed him, and believed, too, that he should have been convicted of manslaughter, not murder, and his life spared.

One of those was Maidstone Prison Governor James Newham, who recorded in his diary: 'In my opinion and that of many others, including Mr F. Scudamore (the under-sheriff) and other lawyers, the wretched man's crime amounted to manslaughter only. The culprit maintained to the last that he did not intend to kill the woman.'

The governor was a compassionate man who by his own account had not been among the witnesses to an execution in all the 25 years he had held office in the prison.

It was his duty to see Fordred pinioned by the executioner, William Marwood, and he recorded afterwards that when the job was done, Fordred told him: 'It's tight enough. No fear of my running away now.'

The execution took place on April 4, 1876. The executioner, Marwood, was a cobbler at Horncastle in Lincolnshire; a man of middle height, broad-shouldered, who habitually dressed in the manner of a Lincolnshire farmer with a high black stock and a low felt hat. He used ropes made specially to his own order in Government workshops.

Before his arrival at Maidstone on this occasion, he wrote to the prison governor asking for improvements to be made to the drop.

His letter, which was not a model of literacy, requested:

'Pleas will you take three feet Squair in the Senter of the Pitt and three feet Deep if this be don it will make a great improvement in the Execution you may depend on me to arive on Monday April the 3rd Day.

'Sir, I Remain your Humble Servant Wm Marwood.'

The improvements were duly carried out and the execution was witnessed by the under-sheriff, F. Scudamore, prisons officers (but not the governor), reporters for *The Times* and other newspapers, the Earl of Lewes and Lord Nevill, son of the Marquis of Abergavenny.

As the rope was adjusted around his neck, Forwood protested: 'Don't choke me!' Those were his last words and they held a certain tragic irony. Executions performed by Marwood's predecessor, a man called Calcraft, were notorious for the way many of his victims choked to death instead of dying instantly.

Despite the 'improvements' to the drop ordered by Marwood, he seems to have performed no better. A reporter for *The Maidstone and Kent Journal* who was among those present at Fordred's death, reported bleakly: 'The culprit struggled for about three minutes.'

THE BRIDE
IN THE BATH

T HE most spectacular of Kent murders in modern times was
certainly that which was committed in the north Kent
seaside resort of Herne Bay in 1912 and which was to
become notorious as the first of the 'Bride in the Bath' series of
murders committed by George Joseph Smith.

Smith earned the rare distinction of a place in Madame Tussaud's in London as a result of his conviction.

His victim at Herne Bay was an unfortunate woman named
Bessie Mundy, who first met Smith – although then she knew him
as Henry Williams – in 1910 in Weymouth.

He was, in her estimation, a pleasant enough youngish man in
his mid 30s. She was a woman of comfortable means, her father
having died in 1904 leaving her £2,500 in a trust fund that paid
her £8 a month. Not a fortune exactly, but a comfortable sum.

Williams, as he then was, made himself agreeable to Bessie, who
responded encouragingly, so that it was not very long before he
had proposed marriage and she had accepted.

Before they were actually married however, Williams told Bessie
about his ambition to start up in business on his own and he took
steps to gain control of her money.

He persuaded her to agree to instruct a Weymouth solicitor to
write to the family solicitor asking for a copy of her father's will
and he wrote to her uncle, who actually controlled the trust fund,
saying it was Bessie's wish that as much of the money to which
she was entitled under the trust terms should be forwarded to
him, Williams.

Bessie's uncle was distinctly uneasy about the request but Bessie was entitled to draw whatever money she wanted from the fund and so he sent a cheque for £135 2s 11d.

Williams cashed the cheque and then accused his new bride of being responsible for his contracting a venereal disease that meant he would have to go away for treatment.

She, of course, was distraught, both at the accusation and at the consequences which he explained would probably mean he would be away for some months in London.

Tearfully, she asked how could she explain to her uncle what had happened to the £135 he had sent her? Williams had an easy answer to that.

'Tell him you put the money in your handbag, which you had with you when you fell asleep on the beach and when you woke up it was gone,' he suggested.

'You had better make up some story of that kind, at any rate, because if you don't there will be police inquiries and then the fact that you have infected me, as you have, will be made public and you will have to face up to the disgrace.'

Poor Bessie. She had only the very haziest understanding of what she was being accused of and she dared not ask anyone else. So she made what excuses came to mind when she was asked what had become of her husband after he left her to pay the rent for their lodgings and went out of her life completely for the next couple of years.

Although she did not know it, Williams in fact returned to a woman called Edith Pegler, who he had 'married' in Bristol before he met Bessie, undeterred by the fact that he was, even before that, married legally to Caroline Thornhill, from whom he had parted in 1905.

Bessie, in her distress, went to live with her brother George, until she felt able to put the whole unhappy episode behind her and begin to reshape her life again.

It would have been better for her if that had been the end of the affair, as it seemed to be. But it was not. Two years later she was living alone in Weston-super-Mare when by pure chance (it would seem) she again met the man she still believed was her lawful wedded husband, Henry Williams.

That meeting sealed her fate. At the time she was delighted to see him again. He was his old agreeable self, apparently fully recovered from his 'illness' and prepared to let bygones be bygones. Within hours of their reunion, she was speaking of him in public in the most affectionate terms, introducing him to friends and acquaintances as her husband.

It was not long before Williams was writing to her brother, George Mundy, to let him know that he and Bessie were reunited and resolved to resume their married life where it was so abruptly interrupted two years before.

He wrote: 'Time is a great healer. Bessie and I are living together again and she has told her friends she is delighted to be with me once more.'

The couple went to live in Herne Bay in Kent, where they rented a small house at 80 High Street. They furnished it, with prudent economy, from the local shops and one of their purchases was a zinc bath, about five ft long, with four little legs, which they installed in the only bedroom in the house.

It represented a small luxury and it would have cost Williams £2 if he had not been able to bargain with the ironmonger who sold it to them and eventually settled on a price of £1 17s 6d, to be paid after an agreed period during which they would take it 'on approval'.

In Herne Bay, Williams let it be known that he was an antiques and art dealer. He and Bessie both made wills in favour of each other, each leaving everything to the other. In fact Bessie was well aware that her husband had very little to leave to her if he died first, but that did not seem to concern her particularly.

As soon as the wills were made, Williams decided his wife needed to see a doctor and he took her to the local Dr French saying that Bessie had suffered some kind of fit. Bessie was very worried because she had no recollection of having had any fit of any kind.

Dr French examined her and reached the conclusion that she was in good health and that the 'fit' must have been a one-off that was unlikely to recur.

Later, during the same week however, Williams sent for the doctor to come to the house where, he said, Bessie had suffered

The seafront at Herne Bay in 1912, when Henry Williams (George Joseph Smith) and Bessie Mundy lived there.

another fit. The doctor came, again examined Bessie and concluded that, despite the fact that she admitted to having a headache, there was no evidence that she had, in fact, had a fit and no reason to suppose there was anything wrong with her general health.

Dr French was well used to ladies whose life-style left them with too much time to worry about their health. Herne Bay was a minor seaside spa town and quite a lot of his patients were hypochondriacs. He assumed he had just added another to his list, advised as much rest as possible, and left the house.

But just after 8am on July 13, 1912, Dr French received a note sent by hand from Williams. It said simply: 'Can you come at once. I'm afraid my wife is dead.'

Of course, Dr French went to the house in the High Street as quickly as he could. He found it difficult to believe that the woman he had so recently examined and found to be perfectly healthy could have died so suddenly.

He was received at the house by Williams and was taken upstairs to the bedroom where Bessie lay, face up, in the bath full of water. Her feet were resting on the rim of the foot of the bath, which was about eight inches shorter than she was. The rest of her body, including her mouth, was under water.

She was, undeniably, dead.

Williams told the doctor that he and his wife had both got up that morning at about 7.30 and he had left the house to go and buy some fish. When he returned, he said, he found his wife as she was now.

Dr French was puzzled. If what he was being told was true, Bessie – who was supposed to suffer from inexplicable fits – had been up and down the stairs about 20 times with buckets of hot water to fill the bath in the time between getting out of bed at 7.30 and the time her husband returned from his shopping expedition and found her, dead, in the bath. Since Williams' note to the doctor was written shortly after 8am, it allowed only about half an hour for the water to have been heated and carried upstairs and for Bessie to have got into the bath and to then die, virtually instantly.

It was perfectly possible but it was, well, unusual.

The doctor was also a bit puzzled about how a woman, who presumably had suffered another of her 'fits' in the bath, could have ended up in the position in which she was found. If she had lost consciousness and simply slipped under the water, surely the most likely position for her would have been with her feet in the bath and her knees up, above the surface of the water.

However, despite his puzzlement, an inquest was held and a verdict of death by misadventure was returned. A death certificate was duly signed and Bessie was buried.

Although the journalistic label was not to be attached until some time later, Bessie Mundy had become the first of the 'Bride in the Bath' victims of murderer George Joseph Smith.

For Henry Williams was not the real name of the man Bessie had believed she was married to. In the course of a few years he used a number of names, including Love, Smith, Williams, Lloyd and James.

He 'married' at least seven women, of whom Bessie was the

third, and three of them, including Bessie, died in their baths. The others lived. But Bessie was his first known victim and it was for her murder alone that he was finally brought to justice.

Dr French was not the only one to entertain suspicions about the manner of her death. Bessie's family had never taken her husband to their hearts and they were distinctly uneasy about the whole affair. However there was nothing they could do to prevent his inheriting her property under the terms of the will that she had made in his favour.

Williams stuck to his story that his wife had suffered a fit while taking a bath. He told it to their landlady, who later recalled that he had added, with what she regarded as very dubious good taste: 'Wasn't it a jolly good job I got her to make a will?'

He lost no time in returning the bath to the local ironmonger, thus avoiding paying for it under the 'on approval' terms of their agreement and he sold the furniture they had bought for the house. As soon as he could, he quit the house in Herne Bay, wrote to Edith Pegler asking her to join him, and spent the next two months with her in Margate before he left her again to embark upon another 'marriage'.

He drew 14 cheques for large sums of money from the cash he inherited from Bessie and bought seven houses in Bristol, later selling them for less than he paid for them.

In the next three years he 'married' four more times. Two of the women, Alice Burham and Margaret Lofty, died in their baths, Alice at Blackpool on December 12, 1913 and Margaret at Highgate, on December 18, 1914.

By this time he was 43 years old and suspicions were well and truly aroused. In June 1915 he was charged in the name of George Joseph Smith with the murder of Beatrice Constance Annie Mundy at Herne Bay on July 13, 1912.

The Old Bailey trial lasted nine days. Evidence was given that the simplest way to drown someone in a bath was to pull the feet forward and hold them there, making it impossible for the victim to struggle free.

In his summing up, the judge, Mr Justice Scrutton, described the murder as cold-blooded and heartless and the murderer as a man on whom exhortations of repentance would be wasted.

The wax figure of George Smith which has chilled visitors to the Chamber of Horrors at Madame Tussaud's since it was first displayed in 1916. (Reproduced by permission of Madame Tussaud's.)

Several times during the trial, Smith interrupted with such comments as: 'You might as well hang me today!' and: 'I am no murderer, though I may be a bit peculiar.'

The jury took just 18 minutes to find him guilty as charged and, asked if he had anything to say, Smith only replied: 'I can only say I am not guilty.'

An appeal was made on his behalf but it failed and sentence of death was duly carried out at Maidstone prison at 8am on Friday, August 13, 1915.

Despite the inauspicious date, it was one of the few really fine days of that summer. When the execution had taken place, there was no traditional tolling of the prison bell and no hoisting of the black flag over the prison gates to tell the public that the deed was done.

It was, of course, in the middle of the First World War and for the first time representatives of the press were not allowed to witness the execution. Local journalists were indignant about that and regarded it as a very unsatisfactory way to conduct a hanging.

Nor was there even the usual notification to the press of the inquest and those journalists who did find out about it were not, as they always had been, permitted to view the body.

That aroused suspicions in the public mind that something had happened at the execution that the prison authorities did not wish to be disclosed. London photographers who arrived to take pictures outside the gaol were hustled off to the local police station, where they were reminded that Maidstone was a wartime prohibited area in which it would have been an offence to take pictures anyway. The Fleet Street pressmen returned to London without the pictures they had been sent to take.

Very soon, the public interest in the fate of multi-murderer and bigamist George Joseph Smith waned as murder on an incomparably greater scale in France took up most of the available news space.

But he remains one of the leading figures in the history of murder in Britain and his crime in Herne Bay is commemorated in the Chamber of Horrors of Madame Tussaud's in London, where his infamy has been preserved in wax since 1916.

Index

Adams, John 32
Allen, John 94
Anderson, James 46
Andrews, John 67, 72
Arden, Alice 8
Arden, Thomas 7
Attwood, Elizabeth 41

Back, Caroline 39
Back, John and Mary 39
Back, Maria 39
Baden Powell, Lord 11
Baker, Stephen 19
Bannister, Govener C.W. 87, 108
Barton, Charlotte 50
Becket, Archbishop Thomas 7
Bell, John Any Bird 11
Bennett, Lt 18
Benstead, Richard 27
Bethlam Hospital 36
Biggs, George 31
Blanchard, George 19
Bligh, Mr 47
Black Will 9
Bossenden 17
Bossenden Farm, Dunkirk 17
Boughton Under Blean 16
Boxley 62

Boyle, James 99
Bradshaw, George 9
Bridger, Mary Ann 109
Brompton 62
Broadmooor Hospital 37
Burford, William 19
Burham, Alice 121
Burton, Robert Alexander 67
Bushell, Henry 26

Calcraft, Executioner William 45, 57, 106, 115
Cambridge Arms, Canterbury 55
Canterbury 16, 53
Canterbury Observer, The 58
Capital Punishment Act, 1868 11
Carter, Mrs 53
Cary, Edmund 94
Chapman, Henry 24
Charing 25
Chatham 30
Chatham Lines, Gillingham 67
Clarke, Mr 71
Clift, William 68
Cobham 30
Cobham Woods 30

Coleshill 26
Coram, Superintendent 51
Courtenay, Lord Viscount
    William
    (see also Thom, 'Mad'
      John) 14
Cox, Superintendent Henry
    102
Crowe, Edward 22
Crown inn, Rochester 35
Curling, Edward 19, 21

Dadd, Richard 32
Dadd, Robert 32
Dark Sun inn, The, Chatham
    71
Dawes, Constable William 31
Denman, Lord 19
Davey, Richard 96
Dover 47
Dover Harbour Station 104
Dover Priory Station 102
Drayson, Police Constable 84
Dudlow, County Coroner J.N.
    108
Dulvey, Dr James 87
Dunkirk 18
Dunkirk church 22

Eaglington, Miss 91
Earl of Lewes 115
Eastling 17
Edwards, Daniel and Mary
    Ann 59
Edwards, George 57, 59
Edwards, Samuel 59
Edwards, Thomas 59
Edwards, Thomas (uncle) 62

Ellis, Adelaide 82
Ellis, William 82
Embury, Police
    Superintendent 95
Emptage, Ann 110
Emptage, George 110
Epps, Police Constable James
    56
Evenden, Richard 72
Everist, Superintendent
    Thomas 69

Faversham 7
Fayle, Dr 73
Fisher, Police Sergeant 69
Fletcher, James 98, 99
Foad, Alexander 19, 21
Fordred, Thomas 109
Foreman, Richard 19, 21
Forwood, Emily 77
Forwood, Mary 76
Forwood, Stephen 76
Foster, William 19
Fox, Stephen 53
Frazer, Sugden 106
Frazer, Rev. W 108
French, Dr 118
French, Stephen 73
Fry, Mr F. 87
Fryer, Constable 42
Furley, Under Sheriff R. 108

Giles, Hannah 23
Giles, Jane 24
Giles, Stephen 24
Golding, John 105
Goodwin, James 19
Graveney Church 17

Green, John 8
Grey, Home Secretary Sir
    George 45, 65
Griggs, George 19, 21
Griggs, Thomas 19
Gurley, Thomas 41
Gurney, Edward 54

Hadley, Edward and Harriet
    53
Hadley, Mary Ann 53
Hadlow, Henry 19
Hadlow Mrs 21
Handley, Rev C.R. 22
Harold, Edward 73
Harris, Ann 24
Harvey, Phineas 19
Herne Bay 116
Hernhill 22
Hibberd, PC Stanley 70
Highams, Walker 90
Hill, Governor 85
Hills, Charles 19, 21
Houghton, Geroge 69
Houghton, Thomas 68

Irons, Police Constable 48

Jenkins, Henry 23, 25

Kent County Constabulary 12
Kentish Advertiser 66
King, Frances 61
Kitham, Richard 41
Knott, Rev Joseph 64

Lawrence, Ann 90
Lawrence, Fr 44

Lawrence, Jeremiah 90
Lawrence, Stephen 90
Lester, Abraham 30
Lester, Charles 30
Liverpool, Charles 30
Liverpool Arms 109
Lock, George 69
Lofty, Margaret 121
Lower Hardres 41

Maidman, Eliza 81
Maidstone 9, 59, 90
Maidstone and Kent Journal
    115
Maidstone County Gaol 9
Maidstone Journal 66, 89
Margate 109
Marsham, Viscount 27
Marwood, Executioner
    William 115
May, Police Constable 95
Mears, Constable John 17
Mears, Nicholas 17
Mears, Thomas 19, 21
Mellor, Mr Justice 87
Mitchell, Elizabeth 48
Mitchell, John 48, 103
Mosby, Thomas 8
Mundy, Bessie 116

Napier Arms, Chatham 69
Neville, Lord 115
Newham, Governor James
    114
Nutting, William 19

Otterden 23

Peach, Constable Richard 26
Pegler, Edith 117
Penenden Heath 10
Phillips, Sir Thomas 33
Prescott, John 103
Price, William 19

Ramsgate 76
Redanies, Dedea 38, 59
Reynold's News 65
Roberts, Elizabeth 24
Robins, Mr 52
Rochester 30
Russell, Lord John 22
Ruxton, Captain John Hay 13
Rye, William 19

St Lawrence 76
St Mary's Isle, Chatham 99
Salmstone Farm, Margate 110
Sanderson, Michael 9
Sandwich Gaol 85
Schmidt, Lieutenant 42
Scudamore, Under Sheriff F.
  114
Scrutton, Mr Justice 121
Seager, Samuel 23
Selling 17
Sessions House, Maidstone 10
Sheldwich Lees 17
Shuttleworth, Charles 26
Ship inn, Cobham 32
Shorncliffe 38
Silk, John 19
Sinclair, Charles 104
Smith, George 106
Smith, George Joseph 116

Smith, Police Constable
  Thomas 63
Sonds, Freeman 66
Southey, Ernest (see Forwood,
  Stephen) 76
Spratt, John 19
Stafford, Elizabeth 9
Stansfield 23
Starr's Coffee House, Holborn
  81
Steddy Hole, Folkestone 41
Stevens, Police Sergeant
  George 105
Strood 30

Taylor, Maria 91
Thom, 'Mad' John
  (see also Courtenay, Lord
    William) 14
Thornhill, Caroline 117
Throwley 17
Tillman, Phillip 72
Times, The 115
Tree, Albert 69
Tussaud's, Madame 116

Valiant Sailor inn, Folkestone
  41
Vigor, Edward 94

Walker, Police Superintendent
  William 42
Wallace, Frances (Fanny) 47
Walshe, Edward Adolphus
  102
Ward, Hon Dudley 78
Waterham Well, Canterbury
  16

Wells, Mr   47
Wells, Thomas   102
White, Josiah   80
White, Mrs   79
White, William   80
Wightman, Mr Justice   74
Wilks, Charles   26

Williams, Henry
   (see also Smith, George
      Joseph)   116
Willis, Mr Justice   106
Wills, William   16, 19, 21
Woolmer, Rev Shirley   74
Wraight Snr, Edward   19, 21
Wraight Jnr, Edward   19, 21